James B. Herndon, Joseph Dommers Vehling, J. W. Ellis

What shall we eat? A manual for housekeepers.

Comprising a bill of fare for breakfast, dinner, and tea, for every day in the year.

With an appendix, containing recipes for pickles and sauces

James B. Herndon, Joseph Dommers Vehling, J. W. Ellis

What shall we eat? A manual for housekeepers.
Comprising a bill of fare for breakfast, dinner, and tea, for every day in the year. With an appendix, containing recipes for pickles and sauces

ISBN/EAN: 9783337823498

Printed in Europe, USA, Canada, Australia, Japan

Cover: Foto ©Andreas Hilbeck / pixelio.de

More available books at **www.hansebooks.com**

WHAT SHALL WE EAT?

A

Manual for Housekeepers.

COMPRISING
A BILL OF FARE FOR BREAKFAST, DINNER, AND TEA, FOR EVERY DAY IN THE YEAR.

WITH AN
APPENDIX,
CONTAINING RECIPES FOR PICKLES AND SAUCES.

NEW YORK:
G. P. PUTNAM & SON, 661 BROADWAY.
1868.

PREFACE.

WHAT SHALL WE EAT?

The design of this Manual is to suggest to ladies, without the trouble of *thinking*, what is seasonable for the table, each day in the week, and how it shall be cooked. Also to present to the community of housekeepers, who sigh over the responsibility of providing for the daily wants of life, an agreeable variety, which may be varied to suit the income of the reader. The receipts have all been tested by actual experience. A daily " bill of fare " for breakfast, dinner, and tea is given, for one week in each month, which will present to the reader at once what is wanted, without the trouble of looking over a cook-book. A collection of Pickles and Sauces of rare merit form a desirable addition at the end.

BREAKFAST.

A word on this early meal. It should be what will best fortify a man for the labor of a long day, and should consist of palatable solids. In a chilly climate like America, wine is a mistake, even with French cookery; if strong, it diminishes business keenness; if weak, it imparts no warmth. Instinct points to hot beverages, either coffee, tea, or chocolate. Every variety of cold meats, game, potted meats, and fish, tongue, boar's head, pickled poultry, etc., are suitable, and with bread form a desirable meal. Omelets, sardines, and roes of different fish, hot buttered cakes, etc., make the eater heavy for the day. There is really no time when one needs so good a supply of food as at breakfast, when one has not eaten for twelve or fourteen hours, and fuel is needed for active existence; yet no meal is so much neglected, and people well informed fritter an appetite away on toast and tea. Fruit is a good digester, dried mango-fish from India, cranberry jam, etc., are all good. A breakfast should be as carefully composed as a dinner. Secure by art what is due to the dignity of the meal, and give it its true position.

INDEX.

	PAGE
A French pie	110
Almond cake	17
" custard	23
" croquantes	92
" pudding	48
Apple Charlotte	101
" dumplings	44
" fritters	40
" jelly	37
" pie	23
" soufflé	86
Apres cake	34
Arrowroot pudding	13
Asparagus soup	68
Barley broth	13
Baked cod's head	83
" Indian pudding	35
" calf's head	79
" batter pudding	92
" mackerel	39
" quince pudding	15
" pike	80
Bakewell pudding	59
Bean soup	30
Beef à-la-mode	49
" collops	56
" patties	10
" soup	11
" ragout	17
Beefsteak pudding	70
Benton tea-cakes	10
Black bean soup	43
Blanc mange	29
Black plum cake	58

	PAGE
Blackberry pudding	84
Boiled perch	109
Boiled beef, sauce piquant	28
Bohemian cream	61
Bolas d'amor	124
Boned lamb	93
Bouilli	93
Bread and butter pudding	91
" cake	53
" pudding	21
Brown biscuit	23
" fricassée	84
" bread ice	57
Bonbons	133
Brandy pudding	47
Boiled pigeons	51
Buns	54
Buckwheat cakes	30
Burnt cream	25
Calves'-foot jelly	97
" liver stewed	26
" brains	72
Carrot pie	106
Caramel custard	15
Candied fruit	133
Celery soup	19
Chicken croquettes	117
" salad	123
" pillau	22
" soup	40
" pot-pie	55
" pudding	74
" à la Carmelite	69
" pie	112

INDEX.

	PAGE
Chicken soup with tomato	20
" patties	13
Chile sauce	130
Cheap soup	109
Champagne cream	86
Chocolate pudding	44
" cream	17
Charlotte Russe	121
Cheese-cakes	121
Clam fritters	126
" soup	27
Croquettes of calf's brains	22
Cranberry and rice jelly	58
Crackers with anchovy sauce	47
" toast	20
Cream fritters	47
" pudding	81
" cake	116
Crème au Marasquin	63
" à la vanille	118
College pudding	26
Cottage soup	118
" pudding	41
Coffee custard	12
" cakes	75
Cocoanut pudding	43
" pie	55
Codling soup	82
Corn meal griddle-cakes	19
" bread	14
" pone	20
Cookies	125
Cold ham cake	16
Curry of chicken	37
Cup-cake	16
Cucumber vinegar	129
" stewed	73
Cutlets of sole	91
Custard cream of chocolate	21
Coloring for jellies	133
Damson pudding	104
Delicate dish	14
Duck with peas	80
Dutch butter	55

	PAGE
Eel soup	95
Fish soup	18
Feather cake	38
Flemish cream	54
Flour pudding	10
French flummery	69
Fricandels of veal	61
Game soup	112
German cake	90
" puffs	31
" toast	53
Gems	27
Ginger cup-cake	21
" pound cake	114
Giblet soup	14
Gloucester pudding	57
Gooseberry pudding	73
Green pea soup	60
Green corn	72
Gravy soup	120
Harrico soup	106
Harrison cake	23
Ham toast	57
" sandwiches	44
Hasty pudding	110
Hock	103
Hot gingerbread	37
Huckleberry pudding	94
Italian cream	60
Ice cream—Newport receipt	82
Irish stew	114
Jelly cake	119
Jersey pickle	129
Kedgeree	75
Kidney fritters	109
" toast	60
Kisses	84
Kringles	44
La Galette cake	122
Lamb's head	41
" " stewed	87
Lemon cheese-cakes	67
" jelly	20
" pudding	69

INDEX.

	PAGE
Lemon syllabub	66
Lobster pie	66
" salad	40
" soup	85
Madeira buns	29
Matrimony	111
Matelote of fish	45
Miroton of apples	38
" of veal	33
Mince pie	29
Macaroni pudding	61
Montagu pudding	52
Mother Eve's pudding	69
Mock turtle soup	24
Mutton kebobbed	39
" kidneys fried	46
" pillau	63
Muffins	21
Mullagatawnee soup	49
Mushroom catsup	130
Marmalades	132
Neat's tongue fricassée	85
New Year's cake	18
New England chowder	48
Orange custard	34
" butter	65
" syrup	133
Oley-cooks	42
Ox-cheek soup	86
Ox-tail soup	115
Oyster soup	9
Orange compote	132
Pea soup	16
Peach pudding	94
Plain cake	28
Plum pudding, not rich	64
" " rich	117
Pigeon pie	43
" fricassée	82
" with peas	62
Pillau of rabbit	97
Pickles and sauces	127
Pickled cauliflower	127
" cucumbers	127

	PAGE
Pickled eggs	127
" lemons	128
" mushrooms	128
" walnuts	128
Potted fish	107
" pigeons	30
Pomme mange	31
Pound-cake	25
" pudding	32
Potatoes à la maître d'hôtel	9
" fritters	110
" soup	123
Preserves and confectionery	131
Quaking pudding	63
Queen cake	56
Ragout of veal	48
Raspberry cream	32
" vinegar	134
Rhenish cream	38
Rice croquettes	71
" custards	45
" griddle-cakes	107
" cake	31
" soup	25
" pudding with fruit	18
Ris de veau	27
Rissoles	65
Roast beef, with Yorkshire pudding	45
Roast ham	98
" lobster	93
Rolypoly pudding	96
Sauce universal	129
Sausage toast	9
Seed cake	110
Scallopped oysters	15
Scot's kail soup	41
Scotch cake	12
Snow cream	59
Soft boiled custard	88
Sponge cake	47
Sponge cake	112
" pudding	107
Spanish fritters	113

INDEX.

	PAGE
Spanish soup	111
Spiced veal	106
Squash pie	12
Stewed eels	119
" chickens	124
" codfish	78
" terrapin	87
" beef	91
" scallops	98
Soup à la Bisque	42
" Julienne	32
" Creci	90
Sago soup	22
Soup à la Flamande	35
" maigre	98
Spring soup	39
Summer soup	74
Swiss pudding	119
Sweetbreads	21
Sweetmeat pudding	67
Strawberry jelly	74
Tapioca pudding	116
Toad-in-a-hole	32
Tipsy pudding	51
Tomato soup	52
" catsup	120
To flavor vinegar	129
To keep grapes in brandy	132
To preserve strawberries in wine	132
To preserve oranges or lemons in jelly	132
To dry cherries without sugar	133
Toffie	133
Transparent pudding	99
Turnip soup	45
Turtle maigre soup	36
Turk's cap	26
Vegetable marrow soup	78
" toast	54
" ragout	75
" soup	70
Veal cutlets with rice	99
" broth	33
" cake	28
Venison soup	113
Vermicelli soup	28
Waffles	11
Walnut vinegar	129
Wheat biscuit	34
White soup	55
Winter soup	124
Whipt cream	79
Winibeg pudding	94

WHAT SHALL WE EAT?

JANUARY.

MONDAY.

Breakfast.—Cold roast beef. Potatoes à la maître d'Hotel. (Boil the potatoes, and cut in thin slices. Take a pint of milk, and when scalding hot, stir in a tablespoonful of butter and flour, rubbed together. Add a small bunch of parsley, chopped fine. When well mixed, throw in the potatoes, shaking carefully without a knife or spoon, to avoid breaking. Salt to taste.) Sausage toast. (Scald the sausages in boiling water, fry to a light brown, chop fine, and spread on buttered toast.) Potted fish. Rolls and butter. Tea and coffee.

DINNER.

Oyster Soup.—Take fifty oysters, strain through a sieve, and put the liquor on the fire. When scalding hot, take $\frac{1}{4}$ lb. of butter, and beat with 6 oz. of flour; roll $\frac{1}{2}$ doz. butter crackers to a powder, and add all to the liquor, with salt and pepper to the taste, and a small pinch of powdered mace. Then add the oysters with a quart of milk (and a gill of cream if you have it), and stir with a silver spoon for ten minutes. Do not let them *boil*, but thoroughly scald.

Boiled Halibut.

Roast Pork.—Serve with apple-sauce, potatoes, and tomatoes. Baste with a little butter and flour, and rub with dried sage crumbed.

Beef Patties.—Chop fine rare roast beef, season with pepper, salt, and a little onion. Make a plain paste, cut into shapes like an apple puff, fill with the mince, and bake quickly.

Dessert.

Flour Pudding.—Five eggs, 1 qt. milk, 4 tablespoonfuls of flour, well stirred together. Bake in a quick oven, and eat with cold sauce.

Fruit and nuts.

Tea, or Lunch, if the Dinner is late.

Cold pickled salmon, tongue, bread and butter, canned peaches, tea and coffee, Benton tea-cakes (1 qt. of flour mixed with milk to a paste, 1 tablespoonful of melted butter. Roll very thin, and bake on hot hearth).

Cream cake (1 lb. flour, 1 lb. sugar, ½ lb. of butter, ½ pt. milk, 4 eggs, citron, raisins, and spice to taste).

TUESDAY.

Breakfast.—Breaded veal cutlet. Fried potatoes. Pickled tripe. Waffles. (Put 2 pints of milk into *separate* pans; warm one slightly, melt in it ¼ lb. of butter, and set it away to cool. Beat 8 eggs, and mix with the other pan, stirring in gradually ½ lb. of flour, and a little salt. Then mix the contents of both pans together, and add a large tablespoonful of yeast. Set near the fire to rise. When quite light, heat the waffle-iron and butter it, pour in the batter, and when done one side, turn. Send to the table hot, six on a plate, buttered, and strewn with powdered sugar if desired.) Hot brown bread. Cold bread. Tea and coffee.

DINNER.

Beef Soup.—Take a shank bone, with part of the leg, and put in a kettle with soft water to cover it, with a small piece of butter to keep from burning, while the juices are extracting. Set on the back of the range, and cook slowly for six hours, then strain, and when *cold*, remove every particle of fat. Place in another pot 5 carrots, 5 onions, 1 cup of rice, ½ a bunch of celery, and a small bunch of parsley. In this pot may be placed any bones, or pieces of *cooked* meat. Let them also stew slowly for six hours, then strain through a colander, and add to the soup, with ½ a cup of tomato catsup.

Let *all* come to a boil together, then serve. Use a wooden spoon in stirring. This quantity of soup will suffice a small family for a week, and should be kept in a cool place, in an earthen vessel.

Fresh Cod, boiled, with melted butter.

Roast Chickens, with mashed potatoes, cauliflower, and stewed celery.

Cold Tongue.

Dessert.

Squash Pie.—One qt. of pulp strained through a sieve; boil 1 qt. of milk, and stir the squash into it, with 2 spoonfuls of flour shaken in. Add 2 eggs, and a piece of butter size of an egg. Season to the taste with sugar, cinnamon, and a little salt.

Coffee Custard.—Boil a pint of milk, and pour upon it, while boiling, 2 tablespoonfuls of *whole* coffee, warmed by the fire. Let it cool for an hour, then sweeten, add the yolks of 4 eggs, thicken over the fire (stirring all the time). When thick enough, strain, and fill the glasses.

Grapes, apples, and hickory nuts.

Tea, or Lunch.

Cold roast meat, raw oysters, apple-sauce, French bread and butter. Crackers. Scotch cake. (Stir to a cream 1 lb. of sugar and ¾ lb. of butter, add the juice and grated rind of a lemon, with a wine-glass of brandy.

Beat separately the whites and yolks of 9 eggs, and stir into the cake. Add 1 lb. of sifted flower, and just as it goes into the pan, 1 lb. of stoned raisins.)

WEDNESDAY.

Breakfast.—Hashed chicken on toast. Cold snipe. Mutton chops. Graham rolls. Dry toast. French bread and butter. Chocolate and coffee.

DINNER.

Barley Broth.—Boil gently, for half an hour, ½ pt. of pearl barley in a gallon of water. Take 3 lbs. lamb chops, with fat cut off, and put in a stewpan, with water to cover them. Add any kind of vegetables, carrots, turnips, onions, and celery cut fine. When tender, add to the barley water, and boil slowly 2 hours. Salt and pepper to taste.

Fried Scallops.

Roast Ducks, (scald, to prevent being oily,) with baked potatoes, onions, canned sweet corn, and celery.

Chicken Patties.—Chop fine and season well, and serve in puff paste.

Dessert.

Arrowroot Pudding.—Simmer a pint of milk with a little cinnamon, take a tablepoonsful of arrowroot, mix with cold water, and pour into the milk, stirring all the time. When cold, add 3 eggs well beaten, and stir all together. Bake ½ an hour in a dish lined with puff paste, and grate a little nutmeg on the top.

Delicate Dish.—Beat the whites of 6 eggs, with 2 spoonfuls of currant jelly, to a *solid* froth, so that it will not fall. Serve with cream and powdered sugar.

Grapes, apples, and pecan nuts.

TEA, OR LUNCH.

Stewed oysters, cold game, French bread. Strawberry jam, sponge cake.

THURSDAY.

Breakfast.—Cold boiled ham. Cold roast duck. Omelet, with parsley. Stewed potatoes, with cream. Steamed toast. Corn bread (3 cups of meal, 1 cup of flour, 1 tablespoonful of butter, do. sugar, 1 teaspoonful of soda, 1 qt. of buttermilk, or sour milk, 2 eggs). Tea and coffee.

DINNER.

Giblet Soup.—Scald and clean a set of giblets, stew in a little gravy with 2 onions, a bunch of sweet herbs. 2 glasses of white wine, pepper, and salt. When tender, take them out and strain the broth. Make a stock with 2 lbs. of beef, and 5 pints of water. Skin 2 onions, slice thin, and fry in butter. Add flour to thicken the broth, with majoram and parsley, and stir all into the boiling stock, Boil $\frac{1}{2}$ an hour, pass through a sieve, and put again on the fire, skimming carefully. Add the giblets, 2 glasses of wine, and a little lemon-juice. Season well.

Boiled Striped Bass, melted butter.

Roast leg of Mutton, with boiled potatoes, fried parsnips, boiled hominy, and baked tomatoes.

Scalloped Oysters.—Scald the oysters in their own liquor, take them out with a fork, lay in a deep dish, sprinkling over each one rolled cracker crumbs, pepper and salt, and small pieces of butter. Stir a little butter and flour together, and stir into the liquor; then fill up the dish with it, and brown in the oven.

Dessert.

Baked Quince Pudding.—Scald some quinces till tender, pare, and scrape off the pulp; then strew it with ginger, cinnamon, and sugar. To a pint of milk, or cream, put the yolks of 4 eggs and stir in the quince to a proper consistency. Bake in a dish lined with paste. *Canned* quinces can be used if necessary.

Caramel Custard.—Melt $\frac{1}{4}$ lb. of pounded sugar over a slow fire till it begins to tint, stirring all the time. Boil 1 oz. of isinglass in a pint of milk, and pour it on the caramel, stirring till quite dissolved. Beat 4 eggs and add; then stir over the fire to thicken. Put in a mould, and then set on the ice.

Fruit and nuts.

Tea, or Lunch.

Cold ham cake. (Take ham that may be getting dry, pound finely, with the fat, in a mortar, season with pepper and mixed spice; add clarified butter sufficient to moisten, and place ½ an hour in the oven. Put the mould in warm water a few minutes, that it may turn out well.) Pickled oysters, dry toast, French bread, griddle-cakes, brandy peaches, cup-cake (4 eggs, 4 cups flour, 3 cups powdered sugar, 1 cup butter, 1 cup milk, 1 glass white wine, spices, and a teaspoonful soda). Tea.

FRIDAY.

Breakfast.—Cold roast mutton, pickled pigs' feet, rolls, brown bread cream toast, boiled samp. Tea and coffee.

Dinner.

Pea Soup.—Put 1 qt. split peas into 3 qts. boiling water (first soak the peas over night); boil gently till dissolved, strain through a sieve, and add thyme, sweet marjoram, and some mushroom catsup. A small piece of ham will improve the flavor. Serve with small pieces of fried bread.

Boiled Whitefish.

Roast Turkey.—With stewed potatoes, canned sweet corn, baked sweet potatoes, and cranberry jelly.

Beef Ragout.—Fry 2 lbs. of beef till quite brown, put it into a stewpan with 6 onions, pepper it well, and stew slowly 4 hours. Serve it up with pickled walnuts, gherkins, and capers, just warmed in the gravy.

Dessert.

Apple Pie.

Chocolate Cream.—Scrape into 1 qt. of milk (or cream) 1 oz. of best French chocolate, and add ¼ lb. of sugar. Boil and and mill it. When smooth, take it off, and add the whites of 6 eggs, beaten to a froth. Strain through a sieve, and put in glasses.

Oranges, raisins, and almonds.

Tea, or Lunch.

Cold turkey, roast oysters, cheese, Graham crackers, preserved ginger, tea and chocolate, almond cake (2 oz. blanched bitter almonds, pounded fine; 7 oz. flour, sifted and dried; 10 eggs; 1 pound loaf sugar, powdered and sifted, and a wine-glass of rose-water).

SATURDAY.

Breakfast.—Broiled ham, potted game, chipped potatoes, milk toast, corn bread, tea and coffee.

Dinner.

Fish Soup.—Take one pound each of any fresh water fish—pike, perch, eels, &c.; wash in salt and water, and then stew with carrots, leeks, sweet herbs, and onions, in as much water as will cover them. Stew until all is reduced to a pulp, then strain, and boil an hour, with a little mace, celery, and mushroom catsup, or any high-seasoned sauce.

Fried Clams.

Broiled Beefsteak, with celery, potatoes, and stewed tomatoes.

Broiled Snipe.

Dessert.

Cranberry Tarts.

Rice Pudding, with fruit.—Swell the rice in milk, over the fire, and add pared and quartered apples, with a little currant jelly.

Pears and dates.

Tea, or Lunch.

Cold corn beef, hashed chicken, fried hominy, hot biscuit, raised, cranberry sauce, chocolate, New Year's cake

(3 lbs. flour, 1½ lbs. powdered sugar, 1 lb. butter, 1 pt. milk, with a teaspoonful of soda dissolved in it, juice of a lemon. Cut into shapes to bake).

SUNDAY.

Breakfast.—Corn beef hash, cold snipe, corn meal griddle-cakes (scald half a pint of Indian meal, half a pint dry, do. flour, and stir all into a pint of milk, with a tablespoonful of butter, and one egg. Spread very thin on the griddle). Rolls, dry toast, tea and coffee.

DINNER.

Celery Soup.—Blanch the heads of two bunches of celery in warm water, and put them in a stewpan of broth made from boiled chicken, with a lump of sugar. Boil an hour, until soft enough to pass through a sieve; add a cup of milk, and season to taste.

Roast Beef, with potatoes, beans, tomatoes, and spiced currants.

Oyster Pie.
Cold Boiled Ham.

Dessert.

Apple Puffs.—Pare and core apples, stew until tender, and when cold mix with sugar, grated lemon, and a little quince marmalade. Put in thin paste, and bake ¼ of an hour.

Soft Boiled Custard.

Macaroons, grapes, apples, and figs.

TEA, OR LUNCH.

Broiled smoked salmon, sliced ham, steam toast, Graham crackers, assorted cakes, currant jelly, bread and butter, tea and chocolate.

FEBRUARY.

MONDAY.

Breakfast.—Beefsteak broiled, cold tongue, baked potatoes, cracker toast (made of Boston hard crackers dipped in boiling milk, thickened with butter and flour), corn pone. (Take a pint of meal and scald it, and when cold, add 2 eggs, salt, and a cup of milk. Heat a round cake-pan, and butter well; then put the pone in, and bake $\frac{1}{2}$ an hour with a quick fire). Tea and coffee.

DINNER.

Chicken Soup with Tomato.—Boil an old fowl slowly until it falls to pieces, season with salt, whole pepper, and 2 onions. Stain it, add two cups of tomato, and boil well together.

Frost Fish Fried.

Roast Turkey, with currant jelly, mashed potatoes, and stewed celery.

Sweetbreads.—Parboil them slightly, and fry a light brown, with some mushroom catsup in the gravy.

Dessert.

Custard Cream of Chocolate.—Grate 2 oz. of spiced chocolate into a pint of milk; put into a stewpan, and add the yolks of 6 eggs. Stir over the fire until it thickens.

Bread Pudding.—1 pt. of bread crumbs, covered with milk, cinnamon, and nutmeg. Stir in, when hot, $\frac{1}{4}$ lb. of butter, $\frac{1}{4}$ lb. of sugar, and mix well together. When cool, add 6 eggs, and bake one hour in a deep dish.

Oranges, nuts, and raisins.

TEA, OR LUNCH.

Cold roast veal, sardines, Graham bread, French rolls, preserved pears, tea and chocolate, ginger cup-cake (5 eggs, 2 teacups of molasses, 2 do. brown sugar rolled fine, 2 do. butter, 1 cup of milk, 5 cups flour, $\frac{1}{2}$ cup of powdered allspice and cloves, $\frac{1}{2}$ cup ginger, $\frac{1}{2}$ teaspoonful soda melted in vinegar).

TUESDAY.

Breakfast.—Codfish balls, cold turkey, muffins (1 qt. milk, 2 eggs, 2 spoonfuls of yeast, do. flour, butter size of an egg, melted in the milk, and a little salt. Warm the milk and add the rest; let it rise, and bake on a griddle). Corn bread, rolls, tea and coffee.

Dinner.

Sago Soup.—Take 2 qts. of gravy soup, made of beef, thicken with sago to the consistency of pea soup, and season with catsup.

Codfish, with oyster sauce.

Chicken Pillau, with potatoes, fried parsnips, and stewed celery. (Put a large fat chicken, old or young, into a pot, with 1 carrot, onion, and a sprig of sweet herbs. Boil and skim. When the chicken is half cooked add a pint of tomatoes, cut up (fresh or canned), and a little broken mace. When it is done enough to eat as boiled fowl, take it up; take out the carrot and onion, and measure the liquor. There should be about 3 pints. To each 2½ cups of soup, put 1 of rice, and when it has boiled ten minutes, stir in a piece of butter, size of an egg. Before putting in the rice, pepper and salt the broth, and when it is tender (but not too soft) take it up. Serve in an oval dish, the fowl in the middle of the rice).

Croquettes of Calf's Brains.—Blanch the brains, and beat them up with one or two chopped sage leaves, pepper, salt, a few bread crumbs soaked in milk, and 1 egg. Roll them into balls, and fry a light brown.

Dessert.

Apple Pie.—Pare and quarter apples, scald in sugar and water, and grate the rind of a lemon over them. Add the juice of the lemon, ½ doz. whole cloves, butter size of a walnut, and fill up the dish with the syrup. Use puff paste.

Almond Custard.—One pt. of cream, do. milk, ½ lb. shelled sweet almonds, 2 oz. bitter almonds, 4 tablespoonfuls rose-water, ¼ lb. white sugar, the yolks of 8 eggs, ½ teaspoonful oil of lemon. Blanch the almonds, and pound to a paste, mixing the rose-water with it. Beat the eggs very light, and add with the sugar. Stir all gradually into the cream and milk, and beat well together. Stir on the fire till thick, and when cold, add the whites beaten to a froth.

Figs and pecan nuts.

Tea, or Lunch.

Cold ham, potted fish, Indian griddle-cakes, cheese, brown biscuit (3 quarts Graham flour, put into one of milk and water, with a tablespoonful of butter, a teaspoonful of soda, and a little salt). Preserved pineapple, tea. Harrison cake (5 cups flour, 1½ butter, 2½ sugar, 1 molasses, 1 cream, 4 eggs, 1 lb. raisins, citron, and mixed spice. Bake 3 hours).

WEDNESDAY.

Breakfast.—Broiled liver, cold venison, potato cakes fried, milk toast of Graham bread, rolls, tea and coffee.

Dinner.

Mock Turtle Soup.—Take half a calf's head, fresh, and unstripped of skin, remove the brains, and clean the head carefully in hot water, leaving it in cold water for an hour. Then put it into 6 qts. warm water, with 2 lbs. veal, do. pork, a roasted onion stuck with cloves, a rind of lemon, 2 sliced carrots, a bunch of herbs, and a head of celery. Let it boil slowly 2 hours; then take out the head and pork. Make forcemeat balls of the brains and tongue, break the bones of the head, put all into the soup, and boil 2 hours more. Put into a small stewpan a piece of butter, onions sliced thin, with parsley, thyme, mace, and allspice. Add flour to thicken, and stir into the soup slowly. Boil gently 1 hour more, pass through a sieve, season with salt, cayenne, lemon-juice, and a pint of Madeira wine. Add mushrooms if desired, and serve with lemons cut in quarters.

Fried Eels.

Broiled Woodcock, with squash, sweet potatoes, and hominy.

Boiled Corn Beef.

Dessert.

Cranberry Pie.

Burnt Cream.—Make a rich custard without sugar, flavor with lemon, and when cold, sift white sugar thickly over it, and brown in the oven.

Oranges and grapes.

Tea, or Lunch.

Fried oysters, ham cake, hominy, dry toast, preserved damsons, bread and butter, chocolate, pound cake. (1 lb. flour, do. powdered sugar, 1 lb. butter, 10 eggs, ½ glass of wine, do. brandy, do. rose-water, mixed; 12 drops essence lemon, 1 tablespoonful mixed spice).

THURSDAY.

Breakfast.—Turkey hash, pickled tripe, fried potatoes, buckwheat cakes, brown and white bread, tea and coffee.

Dinner.

Rice Soup.—Make a beef soup, boil 5 hours, then strain and add a cup of rice, same of tomato, pepper, and salt.

Fried Halibut.

Boiled Mutton, caper sauce, with baked potatoes, canned sweet corn, and turnips.

Calf's Liver Stewed.—Cut the liver in pieces, lard nicely, and spread chopped parsley, pepper, and salt over them. Put a small piece of butter well mixed with flour in the bottom of a stewpan, put in the liver, and let it cook gently in its own juices until done.

Dessert.

College Pudding.—Take ½ lb. of grated bread crumbs, suet (chopped fine), and currants; mix with 4 oz. of flour and 1 egg. Beat in a glass of brandy, season with nutmeg, and boil 3 hours in a mould. Serve with cold sauce.

Lemon Jelly.—One qt. calf's foot stock, ½ pt. lemon juice, ¾ lb. of sugar, the rind of 2 lemons cut *thin*, and the whites and shells of 5 eggs. Boil 20 minutes, and throw in a teacup of cold water; then let it boil 5 minutes longer. Take from the fire and let it stand ½ an hour covered close. Then run through a bag till clear.

Apples, nuts, and dates.

Tea, or Lunch.

Cold woodcock, broiled herring, cracker toast, French bread and butter, currant jelly, tea, Turk's cap (1 pint cream, 7 eggs, ½ lb. flour, and salt; bake quickly).

FRIDAY.

Breakfast.—Mutton chops, minced codfish, with egg, stewed potatoes, rice cakes, gems (wheat flour, unbolted, mixed with water and salt, baked in a roll pan on the top of the range), cold bread, tea, and coffee.

DINNER.

Clam Soup.—Strain the clams, and put on the liquor to boil; beat a spoonful of butter and 1 of flour together, with pepper, and stir into cold water; add to the soup with the clams chopped fine, and when nearly done, add a little milk.

Baked Whitefish.

Boiled Turkey, oyster sauce, with potatoes, squash, and sweet corn.

Ris de Veau.—Blanch 3 sweetbreads, and simmer in a well-flavored gravy till quite done. Have ready 3 round trays of oiled paper, and lay them in, lightly wetted with gravy, fine crumbs of bread, pepper, salt, and a little nutmeg. Do slowly on a gridiron, and serve in the cases.

Dessert.

Peach Pie.
Fancy Cakes.
Figs, nuts, and prunes.

Tea, or Lunch.

Veal cake. (Bone a breast of veal, and cut in slices cut also slices of ham, and boil 6 eggs hard; butter a deep pan, and place all in layers, one over the other, cutting the eggs in slices, and seasoning with cayenne, chopped herbs, anchovy, or any high-flavored sauce. Cover, and bake 4 hours, and when taken from the oven lay a weight upon it; when cold, turn it out.) Cold roast beef, English pickles, crackers assorted, strawberry jam, rolls, plain cake (4 lbs. flour, 2 lbs. currants, and ½ lb. of butter, with clove, carraway seeds, and lemon peel, grated to the taste. Wet with milk, and ½ pt. yeast).

SATURDAY.

Breakfast.—Venison steak, cold boiled mutton, waffles, Indian banock, bread and butter, cocoa and coffee

Dinner.

Vermicelli Soup.—Plain beef, without vegetables; when strained, add vermicelli.

Striped Bass, Broiled.

Boiled Beef, sauce piquant, with tomatoes, potatoes, and parsnips, boiled.

Boil the *rump* slowly for 5 hours; make a strong

gravy of veal, ham, 2 spoonfuls of vinegar, parsley, cloves, onions, and herbs. Strain, and add mushrooms, capers, and a glass of brandy.

Grouse Roasted.

Dessert.

Mince Pie.—Take 2 lbs. of beef chopped fine, 2 lbs. stoned raisins, 2 lbs. currants, 1 lb. sultana raisins, 2 lbs. apples, ¾ lb. sugar, 2 lbs. suet, the juice of 2 lemons, and the rind of 1 chopped fine, ¼ lb. of mixed spice, 2 glasses of brandy, 2 oz. of citron, and 2 of candied lemon peel. Mix well together in a jar. It will improve by lying a few days. Use puff paste.

Blanc Mange.—Boil 1½ oz. of isinglass, 3 oz. of sweet and 6 oz. of bitter almonds, (well pounded,) in a quart of milk. Sweeten, strain through a napkin, and put in the mould.

Fruit and nuts.

TEA, OR LUNCH.

Cold boiled turkey, scalloped oysters. (Dry the oysters with a cloth, and spread in layers in a deep dish, sprinkling each layer with pepper and salt, butter, and bread crumbs or rolled cracker. Bake 20 minutes.) Muffins, bread and butter, raspberry jam, Madeira buns (beat 8 oz. of butter to a cream, and add 2 eggs; take 14 oz. of flour, 6 of white sugar, ½ nutmeg, one teaspoonful ginger, and a spoonful of carraway seeds. Mix and work into the butter, and beat $\frac{1}{2}$ an hour. Add a wineglass of sherry, and bake quick in patty pans). Tea.

SUNDAY.

Breakfast.—Liver hash, cold grouse, chipped potatoes, gems of cornmeal, brown bread milk toast, buckwheat cakes. (To 3 pts. of buckwheat flour mixed into a batter, add one teaspoonful of carbonate of soda, and one of tartaric acid dissolved in water. Bake at once.) Tea and coffee.

DINNER.

Bean Soup —Soak a pint of small white beans over night, boil slowly 3 hours, adding a small piece of ham when half done. Season well, and strain.

Hard-shell Crabs.

Roast Beef, with rice, sweet potatoes, and baked tomatoes.

Potted Pigeons.—Stew the gizzards and livers, chopped fine; add grated ham, bread crumbs, and herbs. Make into a forcemeat, rolling it round the yolk of a hard-boiled egg, and stuff the pigeons. Put into a stewpan with water and a little butter; add gravy of the gizzards, a little flour, and an onion. Stew gently until done, adding a glass of wine.

Dessert.

German Puffs.—Put ½ lb. of butter into ½ a pt. of milk, and when it boils add a cup of flour; beat well together, and when cold add 6 eggs well beaten, with ½ cup of sugar, and grated lemon. Bake in a moderate oven.

Pomme Mange.—Peel and core 1 lb. of apples, and add to ¼ lb. of sugar and ½ pt. of water. Boil till quite stiff, with some lemon peel. Put in a mould.

Oranges, bananas, and nuts.

Tea, or Lunch.

Cold lamb, smoked salmon, broiled. Graham dry toast, cheese, milk biscuit, preserved grapes, rice cake (1 lb. ground rice, do lump sugar sifted, 8 eggs well beaten, the rind of a lemon. Beat all half an hour; and bake 1½ hours). Tea.

MARCH.

MONDAY.

Breakfast.—Boiled eggs, toast, breaded lamb chops, fried potatoes, pickled tripe, corn bread, rolls. Tea and coffee.

Dinner.

Soup à la Julienne.—Cut in pieces size of dice 1 head of celery, 2 carrots, 2 turnips, some small button onions, heads of asparagus (dried) and hearts of lettuce. Boil slowly, and add to a beef broth. Use neither pepper or catsup.

Blackfish, boiled, melted butter.

Roast Veal, with potatoes stewed, cauliflower, and tomatoes.

Toad-in-a-hole.—Make a common batter of eggs, flour, and milk, rather thick, and put in the centre a fowl boned and stuffed with forcemeat; cover entirely with batter, and bake it. (Any kind of meat may be dressed in the same manner.)

Dessert.

Pound Cake Pudding.—One pt. flour, 1 cup milk, do. sugar, do. butter, 2 teaspoonfuls cream of tartar, sifted in the flour, 1 of soda (dissolved in the milk), 3 eggs. Bake 1 hour, and serve with wine sauce.

Raspberry Cream.—Put ½ oz. isinglass, dissolved in water, into a pint of cream, sweetened to the taste; boil it. When nearly cold, lay some raspberry jam in a glass dish, and pour the cream over it.

Bananas, pecans, and figs.

Tea, or Lunch.

Cold Turkey, pickled salmon, fried clams, crackers and cheese, toast, peach sauce. Prune tartlets.

TUESDAY.

Breakfast.—Poached eggs on toast, hashed veal, cold snipe, chipped potatoes, Graham rolls, bread, chocolate and coffee.

Dinner.

Veal Broth.—4 lbs. scrag of veal, and a bunch of sweet herbs, simmer in 6 qts. of water; when half done skim, and add an onion. Add 2 oz. rice, parsley, celery, pepper, and salt.

Fresh Mackerel, broiled.

Boiled Leg of Lamb.—Caper sauce, with fried parsnips, hominy, sweet corn, and potatoes.

Miroton of Veal.—Chop very fine cold dressed veal and ham, mix with a slice of bread soaked in milk, and squeezed dry, 2 onions chopped and browned, salt, pepper, and a little cream. Put all into a stewpan until hot, and well mixed, then add 1 or 2 eggs, butter a mould, and bake until it is brown. Serve with fresh gravy.

Dessert.

Winibeg Pudding.—Pound and sift 5 crackers, and mix with a cup of boiling water, one of sugar, and the juice and peel of a lemon. Bake in a crust.

Orange Custard.—The juice of 6 oranges, strained, and sweetened with loaf sugar; stir over a slow fire till the sugar is dissolved, taking off the scum; when nearly cold add the yolks of 6 eggs well beaten, and a pint of cream (or milk.) Stir over the fire till it thickens, and serve in glasses. Double the quantity if required.

Filberts, oranges, and raisins.

Tea, or Lunch.

Broiled oysters, ham cake, cold lamb, rolls, wheat biscuit, (1 pt. sour milk, 1 teaspoonful soda, do. salt, ½ cup molasses, thicken with wheat meal. Take out enough for a biscuit with a spoon, and roll gently in flour.) Dried apple sauce, Apees cake, (1 lb. flour, ½ lb. butter, do. powdered sugar, ¼ glass of wine, a teaspoonful cinnamon, cloves, and allspice, 3 of carraway seeds,) tea, and chocolate.

WEDNESDAY.

Breakfast.—Omelet with parsley, cold boiled ham, mutton chops, stewed potatoes, steam toast, corn bread, tea and coffee, rolls.

Dinner.

Soupe à la Flamande.—Take 2 carrots, turnips, and onions, a small quantity of celery and lettuce, shred them in pieces, and stew slowly till tender with a teacup of gravy and a piece of butter. Then add a qt. of any sort of broth, and stew gently for an hour with salt, mace, a little sugar, and cayenne. Mix the yolks of 3 eggs well with ½ pt. of cream, (or milk,) and stir in just before it is served.

Smelts.

Roast Beef.—With beets, mashed potatoes, stewed celery, and canned tomatoes.

Oyster Patties.

Dessert.

Baked Indian Pudding.—Take 6 eggs to 1 qt. milk, and 3 tablespoonfuls of meal. Bake ½ an hour. Boiled molasses sauce.

Brandy Cherries.

Macaroons.

Oranges, and candied fruits.

Tea, or Lunch.

Game pâté, veal cake, sardines, waffles, bread, jelly cake, grape jelly, plum cake, chocolate.

THURSDAY.

Breakfast.—Ham and eggs, cold beef, pickled pigs' feet, buckwheat cakes, rolls, cream toast Graham, tea and coffee.

DINNER.

Turtle Maigre Soup.—Use the turtle flesh (preserved in jars in a state of jelly) stewed up in a vegetable, or fish stock, instead of meat, in sufficient quantity to make it limpid. Season with Madeira wine, lemon, thyme, marjoram, and parsley; also nutmeg, allspice, mace, cloves, pepper, and salt, ½ teaspoonful of curry powder, and a few truffles.

Fried Porgies.

Roast Canvass-back Ducks, with onions, sweet corn, carrots, and potatoes.

Fried Sweetbreads.

Dessert.

Apple Pie.

Champagne Cream.—Beat the yolks of 6 eggs with powdered sugar till stiff, pour over it gradually, stewing all the time, a bottle of champagne cream. Cider will also do.

Bananas, oranges, and pecans.

TEA, OR LUNCH.

Cold chicken, Pâté de fois gras, olives, steam toast,

Graham bread, French bread, apple jelly, (pour 1 qt. of apple juice on 1 lb. fresh apples pared and cored, simmer till well broken, strain off the juice, and let it stand till cold. Then add 2 oz. isinglass, 9 oz. sugar, 2 lemons, rind and juice, and whites and shells of 8 eggs. Let it boil $\frac{1}{4}$ of an hour, strain, and put in a mould), hot gingerbread, (1 pt. molasses, do. sour milk, $\frac{2}{3}$ of a cup butter, a spoonful of ginger, and a little salt. Mix thick as cake), tea.

FRIDAY.

Breakfast.—Lamb chops, clam fritters, scrambled eggs, milk toast, corn bread, rolls, tea, and coffee.

Dinner.

Oyster Soup.—Given in January.

Boiled Halibut, melted butter.

Curry of Chicken, with rice, squash, and turnips.

Cut up a raw chicken, put it in a stewpan with 2 oz. of butter, $\frac{1}{2}$ an onion sliced thin, a few sprigs of parsley and thyme, and 2 oz. lean ham; let the whole stew gently a few minutes. Add a large spoonful curry powder, and a small one of flour. Shake the whole 5 minutes over the fire, then put to it a pint of gravy or water; let the whole simmer till the chicken is done, then take it out, and rub the sauce through a sieve, boil it up, skim, and season well.

Veal Patties.

Dessert.

Miroton of Apples.—Scald the apples, reduce to a pulp, and pile high on the dish in which they are to be served; boil 1 teaspoonful of grated lemon-peel, and 6 or 8 lumps of sugar in a teacup of water; then add the yolks of 3 eggs, and the white of 1, ½ oz. butter, a spoonful of flour, and 1 of brandy, mix the whole over the fire, and stir quite smooth. Pour it on the apples, then whisk the whites of the other 2 eggs to a froth, put them over the miroton just as it is going into the oven, and sift some sugar over it. Bake 10 or 15 minutes in a slow oven.

Rhenish Cream.—Dissolve 1 oz. isinglass in 1 pt. hot water, let it stand till cold; take the yolks of 5 eggs, the juice of 3 lemons, ½ pt. white wine, ½ lb. lump sugar. Stir all together, and let them boil gently till thick enough to put into moulds.

Dates, oranges, and nuts.

TEA, OR LUNCH.

Cold stewed pigeons, cold ham, pickled pig's head, muffins, flour griddle-cakes, green grape preserves, feather cake (3 cups raised dough, 2 of sugar, 2 eggs, ½ cup warm milk, 1 cup butter, 1 teaspoonful soda, grate a lemon rind, stand near the fire till light), tea, and chocolate.

SATURDAY.

Breakfast.—Fresh cod fried, fried eggs, pickled tongue, corn beef hash, potatoes à la maitre d' hotel, raised biscuit, toast, tea, and coffee.

DINNER.

Spring Soup.—Take all kinds of green vegetables, asparagus tops, spinach, lettuce, onions, etc., and stew thick in any good broth.

Baked Mackerel.—Take off the heads, clean the fish, and replace the roes, rub with salt, pepper, and allspice. Pack the fish close in a deep baking-pan, cover with equal parts cold vinegar and water, and bake 1 hour in a slow oven.

Mutton Kebobbed.—Cut a loin of mutton into steaks, take off the fat and skin; mix a grated nutmeg with a little salt, pepper, crumbs, and herbs; dip the steaks into the yolks of 3 eggs beaten, and sprinkle the mixture over them. Then place the steaks together as they were before cut, tie, and fasten on a spit, and roast before a quick fire. Set a dish under it, and baste with the liquor and a piece of butter. When done lay in a deep dish, and put over it, ½ pt. gravy, 2 spoonfuls ketchup, and a teaspoonful of flour, first boiled and skimmed.

Lobster Salad.—Mash with a wooden spoon the yolks of 9 eggs boiled hard, mix with ½ pt. sweet oil, (or cream) add 1 gill mixed mustard, ½ teaspoon cayenne, and 1 teaspoon salt. Cut the lobster fine with lettuce, and a few minutes before it is to be eaten, mix the dressing with it thoroughly.

Peach Pie.

Arrowroot Pudding.—1 spoonful of powder mixed in 2 of cold milk; pour on it 1 pt. boiling milk, in which have been dissolved 4 oz. butter and 2 of sugar, stirring well. Add a little nutmeg and 5 eggs, bake ½ an hour in a dish lined with paste.

Oranges, bananas, and Madeira nuts.

Tea, or Lunch.

Potted veal, stewed lobster, cream toast, crackers and cheese, canned pears, rolls, tea. Fancy cakes.

SUNDAY.

Breakfast.—Beefsteak, with mushroom sauce, cold potted pigeons, corn muffins, steam toast, boiled eggs, cold bread. Tea and coffee.

DINNER.

Scots' Kail Soup.—4 lbs. mutton to 1 gallon cold water, and 2 oz. pearl barley; stew until tender, with 2 onions. Have ready the hearts of 2 cabbages chopped fine, put into the broth, and boil uncovered till reduced to 2 qts. Add only pepper and salt.

Flounders Fried.

Roast Partridges.—With spinach, salsify, and potatoes.

Lamb's Head.—Parboil, and rub with the yolk of an egg, cover thickly with herbs, crumbs of bread, butter and put in the oven. Mince the heart and liver, stew in a good gravy, adding a spoonful of ketchup. Make some forcemeat balls, place the mince in a dish with the head upon it, and garnish with the balls, sliced lemon, and pickles.

Dessert.

Cottage Pudding.—Break 1 egg in a pan, add a cup sugar, 1 teaspoon butter, 2 cream of tartar, 1 soda, a cup of milk, and 3 of flour. Pare and slice a lemon, and stir into the batter. Bake $\frac{3}{4}$ of an hour, and eat with cold sauce.

Prune Tarts.

Figs, oranges, and nuts.

Tea, or Lunch.

Cold chicken pie, sardines, cold lamb, hot biscuits, cream toast, crackers and cheese, apple jelly, oleycooks (from Washington Irving,—1 pt. milk, ¼ lb. butter, 2 eggs, 1 tablespoonful brewer's yeast, ½ cup sugar, a little salt and nutmeg. Stand over night till very light, and fry in boiling lard.) Tea and chocolate.

APRIL.

MONDAY.

Breakfast.—Fresh shad broiled, poached eggs, corn bannock, cold roast veal, dry toast, rice cakes, rolls and bread. Tea and coffee.

Dinner.

Soup à la Bisque.—¼ lb. rice, and 12 crabs, (soft shell); boil in good broth, and when done pound, and rub through a sieve. Fill the heads of the crabs with fish stuffing, and add a little butter.

Bluefish Broiled.

Roast Veal, stuffed, with Bermuda potatoes, raw tomatoes dressed, and asparagus.

Lobster Plain.

Dessert.

Jelly Tarts of Puff Paste.

Cocoanut Pudding.—Grate a cocoanut after taking off the brown skin, mix with 3 oz. white powdered sugar, and ½ peel of a lemon; mix well with milk, put in a tin lined with paste, and bake not too brown.

Bananas, and nuts.

Tea, or Lunch.

Veal cake, cold tongue, Graham dry toast, preserved pears, rolls, crackers and cheese, cup cake with almonds.

TUESDAY.

Breakfast.—Veal hash, omelet, stewed potatoes, wheat gems, brown bread cream toast, rolls. Tea, and coffee, potted fish.

Dinner.

Black Bean Soup.—Thicken a strong beef broth, strained, with black beans.

Baked Shad.

Roast Lamb, mint sauce, with baked potatoes, asparagus, and spinach.

Pigeon Pie.—Cut a nice rump steak into small pieces, and cover the bottom of a dish, add seasoning, and sweet herbs. Boil 2 eggs hard, chop the livers fine, add bread crumbs, butter, and seasoning, and stuff the pigeons. Put in with the steak, cover with water or gravy, and bake with a paste.

Dessert.

Apple Dumplings.—1 large apple, quartered, cored, and put together, covered with a thin paste, and boiled till done. As many as are needed, serve with hot sauce.

Chocolate Pudding.—Boil 1 pt. milk, dissolve in it 1 oz. of chocolate, sweeten with loaf sugar, add the yolks of 8, and the whites of 4 eggs well beaten; strain, and pour into a mould, buttered and papered; steam for $\frac{1}{2}$ an hour; let it settle for 10 minutes, and serve with the following sauce: boil $\frac{1}{2}$ stick vanilla in 1 pt. milk till it is reduced one half; strain, sweeten, and thicken with arrowroot.

Figs, and nuts.

Tea, or Lunch.

Ham sandwiches, (chop the ham fine, and season with mustard, pepper, and salt, spread between thin slices buttered bread,) cold game, minced codfish, rolls, toast, stewed prunes, kringles. (Beat well yolks of 8, and whites of 2 eggs, mix with 4 oz. butter, warmed, 1 lb. flour, and 4 oz. sugar to a paste. Roll into thick biscuits, and bake on tin plates.

WEDNESDAY.

Breakfast.—Blue fish, scrambled eggs, baked potatoes, cold chicken, Indian griddle-cakes, rolls, tea and coffee.

Dinner.

Turnip Soup.—Scrape fine 6 large turnips into 2 qts. strong beef soup, with 2 onions fried in butter. Let it simmer slowly, then rub through a sieve till smooth.

Boiled Halibut, oyster sauce.

Roast Beef, with Yorkshire pudding, and vegetables. 1 pt. boiling milk to a small loaf of bread, crumbed fine, 4 eggs, a little salt and flour. Bake in a tin under the drippings of the beef.

Matelote of Fish.—Cut into small pieces any white fish, put into a stewpan with 1 oz. of butter to brown, adding ½ pt. wine, do. good gravy, spice, and seasoning, a sliced carrot and turnip. Take the fish out carefully, keep hot, and thicken the gravy with butter and flour, adding 6 button onions which have been scalded, the same of mushrooms and oysters, lemon-juice, and cayenne. Pour boiling hot on the fish.

Dessert.

Dried Apple Pie.

Rice Custards.—Sweeten a pint of milk, and boil, sifting in ground rice till thick; take off the fire, and add 3 eggs, beaten; stir again over the fire for three minutes, and put into cups that have lain in cold water without wiping. When cold turn out, and pour soft custard around them, with currant jelly on the top of each one.

Prunes, oranges, and candied fruits.

TEA, OR LUNCH.

Mutton kidneys, fried. (Cut in thin slices, flour and fry quickly, serve in good gravy). Roast beef deviled, sardines, apple fritters, (yolks of 6 eggs, whites of 3; beat well and strain, then add 1 pt. milk, a little salt, ½ nutmeg grated, and a glass of brandy. Mix into a thick batter with flour, slice the apples in round, taking out the core, dust with sugar, (let them stand an hour or two) and dip each slice in batter, frying in boiling lard.) Rolls, toast, grape jelly, chocolate.

THURSDAY.

Breakfast.—Codfish balls, fried Indian pudding, boiled eggs, cold lamb, milk toast, rolls, tea, and coffee.

DINNER.

Chicken Soup.—Boiled, strained, with rice and seasoning.

Spanish Mackerel.

Roast Ducks, with asparagus, lettuce, and tomatoes, currant jelly.

Breaded Veal Cutlets.

Dessert.

Brandy Pudding.—Line a mould with stoned raisins or dried cherries, then with thin slices of French roll, next to which put macaroons, then again fruit, rolls, and cakes, till the mould be full, sprinkling in by degrees 2 wine-glasses of brandy. Beat 4 eggs, put to a pint of milk or cream, lightly sweetened, ½ a nutmeg, and the rind of ½ a lemon grated. Let the liquid sink into the solid part, then tie tight with a floured cloth, and boil 1 hour. Keep the mould right side up. Serve with sauce.

Cream Fritters.—One and a half pts. of flour to 1 pt. of milk; beat to a froth with 6 eggs; add 1 pt. cream, ½ nutmeg, a teaspoonful salt, mix well, and fry in small cakes.

Bananas and nuts.

Tea, or Lunch.

Roast oysters, cold miroton of veal, minced fresh fish, Boston crackers, with anchovy sauce, (soak the crackers split in cold water, butter and spread on the sauce thickly.) Muffins, bread, quince marmalade, sponge cake, (1 coffee-cup sugar, do. flour, 4 eggs.) Tea and cocoa.

FRIDAY.

Breakfast.—Shad roes fried brown, omelet with parsley, lamb chops, chipped potatoes, brown bread, rolls, tea and coffee.

Dinner.

New England Chowder.—Fry thin slices of pork in a deep pot; lay in the head and shoulders of a fresh cod, cut in pieces, put in layers, the pork between; season with pepper, salt, and a few cloves; fill up with water and boil; when nearly done add a pint of milk, and 6 Boston crackers split open.

Broiled Shad.

Roast Chickens, with potatoes, asparagus, and tomatoes.

Ragout of Veal.—Fry 2 lbs. of veal till brown, then put into a stew-pan with 6 onions, pepper and mixed spice, add boiling water, and let it stew slowly for 4 hours. Serve with pickled walnuts, or capers, in the gravy.

Dessert.

Almond Pudding.—Two and-a-half oz. white bread crumbs, steeped in a pint of cream, (or milk) ½ pt. blanched almonds pounded to a paste, with a little water, yolks of 6 eggs and whites of 3, beaten; mix all together, and add 3 oz. sugar, and 1 oz. beaten butter. Stir over the fire till thick, and bake in a puff paste.

Blueberry Pie.—Use canned fruit.

Oranges, almonds, and raisins.

TEA, OR LUNCH.

Clam fritters, cold tongue, potted fish, stewed potatoes, hot brown bread, steam toast, preserved plums, buns.

SATURDAY.

Breakfast.—Fresh trout, fried chicken, with cream, water cresses, scrambled eggs, Graham biscuit, corn bread, rolls, tea and coffee.

DINNER.

Mullagatawnee Soup.—Six onions, and $\frac{1}{2}$ lb. butter, pound well, and add 3 spoonfuls curry powder, a little cayenne and salt. Beat all together with some India pickle and flour, and stir into 3 qts. of strong beef soup. Let it boil half an hour, rub through a sieve, and serve with rice.

Baked Bluefish.

Beef à la mode, with turnips, carrots and potatoes. A round of beef, weighing 20 lbs., rub with salt, and tie with tape; chop the marrow from the bone, $\frac{1}{4}$ lb. suet, herbs, thyme, and parsley; add 2 grated nutmegs, ½ oz. cloves, do. mace, tablespoon pepper, do. salt, and 2 glasses Madeira wine; cut 1 lb. pork in small pieces, make incisions in the beef and slip in, then lay in a deep dish, and cover with the seasoning. Bake or stew slowly (with water in the dish) 12 hours. If to be eaten hot, begin the night before. Add wine and a beaten egg in the gravy.

Sweetbreads, fried.

Dessert.

Bread Pudding.—One pt. bread-crumbs, covered with milk, add cinnamon, lemon-peel, and grated nutmeg; put them on a gentle fire until the crumbs are well soaked. Take out the cinnamon, and lemon-peel, beat the milk and crumbs together, add 4 eggs well beaten, 1 oz. butter, 2 oz. sugar, ½ lb. currants, and boil it one hour.

Pine-apples, and macaroons.

Oranges, and nuts.

TEA, OR LUNCH.

Oyster pie, cold corned beef, eggs on toast, cranberry jelly, biscuit, Turk's cap, sponge cake.

SUNDAY.

Breakfast.—Veal chops, with tomato sauce, fried potatoes, cold ham, poached eggs, corn bannock, bread, tea and coffee.

DINNER.

Oyster Soup.

Fried Perch.

Boiled Chicken, with potatoes, asparagus, macaroni, and rice.

Broiled Pigeons.—Cut the pigeons down the back, flatten, and truss. Egg them both sides, season, dip in chopped herbs and crumbs, a little warmed butter sprinkled over them, and broil a light brown.

Dessert.

Tipsy Pudding.—Lay in a dish slices of sponge or pound cake, well soaked in brandy, and pour over them a rich soft custard.

Jam Tarts.

Pine-apples and oranges.

TEA, OR LUNCH.

Cold à la mode beef, broiled ham, mashed potato cakes fried, cheese, crackers, preserves, pound cake with fruit.

MAY.

MONDAY.

Breakfast.—Fried perch, potted game, water-cresses, clam fritters, boiled eggs, rolls, bread, tea, and coffee.

DINNER.

Tomato Soup.—Cut up 2 onions, and fry them in butter; when the onions are brown, add to them a dozen tomatoes, from which you have squeezed the water. Put in a pot with a turnip, 2 lettuces, a piece of lean ham, a stick of celery, some herbs, spice, and a piece of butter. Let it simmer for ½ an hour, stirring occasionally, then fill up with stock, and allow it to boil gently 2 hours. Put in 2 French rolls crumbed, and when done rub through a colander.

Broiled Salmon.

Leg of Lamb boiled, melted butter, with asparagus, potatoes, lettuce, and tomatoes.

Hard-Shell Crabs.

Dessert.

Soft Custards, baked in Paste.

Montagu Pudding.—Half lb. chopped suet, 4 tablespoonfuls of flour, 4 eggs, and 4 spoonfuls of milk mixed into a batter; add ½ lb. stoned raisins, a little sugar, and boil 4 hours.

Pine-apple, bananas, and nuts.

TEA, OR LUNCH.

Fried shad roes, game pâté, German toast. (Take the remainder of a fricassee or ragout, chop fine, add a few herbs with parsley, and mix with 1 or 2 eggs, according to quantity. Put it on the fire with gravy, and let it reduce or thicken. When cold, spread thickly on toast, brush lightly with beaten egg, sprinkle bread-crumbs on each piece, and bake in the oven.) Rolls, bread, sliced pine-apple with sugar, bread cake. (Take raised dough for one loaf, and knead well into it 2 oz. butter, do. sugar, and 8 oz. currants. Warm the butter in a cup of milk.) Tea and chocolate.

TUESDAY.

Breakfast.—Broiled spring chicken, fried potatoes, cold pigeon pie, brown bread, raised biscuit. Tea and coffee.

DINNER.

Veal Broth.—Stew a knuckle of veal, 5 lbs. in 3 qts. water, with an onion, 2 blades of mace, a head of celery, parsley, pepper and salt. Let it simmer gently till reduced to 2 qts. Take out the meat, and serve separately; add 2 oz. boiled rice to the broth.

Baked stuffed Shad.

Breaded Lamb Chops, with asparagus, potatoes, and green peas.

Cold Tongue.

Dessert.

Rhubarb Pie.

Flemish Cream.—Dissolve ½ oz. isinglass in a pint of water, strain it, and add to ½ pt. cream. Add a glass of brandy, color with currant jelly, whisk to a froth, and put into a mould.

Madeira nuts and oranges.

TEA, OR LUNCH.

Cold lamb, lobster salad, sardines, vegetable toast. (Take stewed vegetables, and make it into a purée; add more seasoning, the yolk of an egg, and thicken over the fire. Spread on toast, add bread-crumbs, brush with egg, and bake.) Green gage preserves, buns, (½ lb. flour, ½ lb. sugar, 1 lb. butter, melted in a little warm water, 6 spoonfuls rose water, and ½ pt. yeast. Make a light dough, and add caraway seeds.) Tea and cocoa.

WEDNESDAY.

Breakfast.—Veal chops breaded, broiled shad, stewed potatoes, pickled tongue, water-cresses, rice cake, Graham biscuit, bread. Tea and coffee.

DINNER.

White Soup.—Boil fowls to a jelly, pound the meat in a mortar, and add to the broth. Take 2 qts. of this stock to 4 of water, season, and thicken with 1 lb. rice flour.

Stewed Lobster.

Chicken Pot Pie.—Cut the chicken in small pieces, stew slowly, and thicken the gravy with stirred butter and flour. Make a paste of cream tartar and soda, put on the top, cover tight, and stew ½ an hour.

Boiled Corned beef.

Dessert.

Cocoanut Pie.—Grate the white part, mix with milk, and boil slowly ten minutes; allow 1 qt. milk to 1 lb. cocoanut, 8 eggs, 4 spoonfuls sugar, a glass of wine, a small cracker pounded fine, and 2 spoonfuls melted butter. Bake in deep plates lined with puff paste.

Dutch Butter.—Two oz. isinglass dissolved in a pint of water, with a lemon peel. Add a pint white wine, the juice of 3 lemons, yolks of 8 eggs well beaten, sweeten, make quite hot, and strain into moulds.

Almonds, raisins, and bananas.

TEA, OR LUNCH.

Cold roast veal, corn pone, sweetbreads fried, cheese and assorted crackers, preserved ginger, Queen Cake, (1 lb. powdered sugar, 1 lb. butter, 14 oz. flour, 10 eggs, 1 wine-glass brandy and wine mixed, 12 drops essence of lemon, 1 teaspoonful cinnamon and cloves, and 1 nutmeg.)

THURSDAY.

Breakfast.—Boiled ham and poached eggs, chipped potatoes, cold roast beef, corn bread, water cresses, dry toast, fried shad roes. Tea and coffee.

DINNER.

Sago Soup.—Any white soup thickened with sago.

Broiled Fresh Mackerel.

Roast Lamb, mint sauce, with potatoes, spinach, and raw tomatoes.

Beef Collops.—Cut the inside of a sirloin into circular shapes, the size and thickness of a quarter of a dollar, flour, and fry them; sprinkle with pepper, salt, chopped parsley; make a gravy, and serve with tomato sauce.

Dessert.

Tapioca Pudding.

Brown Bread Ice.—Grate stale brown bread, and soak in cream; sweeten, and freeze.

Bananas and prunes.

Tea, or Lunch.

Ham toast. (Grate or pound cold ham, mix with the yolk of an egg and a little cream, warm over the fire, and serve hot on toast,) corned beef hash, corn bread, crackers, and cheese, stewed prunes, steam toast, macaroons. Tea.

FRIDAY.

Breakfast.—Broiled shad, stewed clams, pickled pig's head, corn muffins, hashed lamb, bread, rolls. Coffee.

Dinner.

Clam Soup.

Bluefish, Broiled.

Stewed Veal, with asparagus, spinach, and potatoes.

Lobster Salad.—Dress like chicken salad.

Dessert.

Gloucester Pudding.—Take 3 eggs, same weight in

butter and flour each, 5 oz. sugar, and 12 bitter almonds powdered, beat well, and bake ½ an hour in cups.

Jelly Tarts.

Fruit and nuts.

TEA, OR LUNCH.

Cold boiled ham, raw oysters, sardines, muffins, toast, preserved damsons, black plum cake. (1 lb. flour, do butter, do. white sugar, 12 eggs, 2 lbs. raisins, 2 lbs. currants, 2 tablespoonfuls mixed spice, 2 nutmegs powdered, a glass wine, brandy, and rose water, and 1 lb. citron.) Tea and chocolate.

SATURDAY.

Breakfast.—Minced veal on toast, cold birds, gems, boiled eggs, brown bread. Tea and coffee.

DINNER.

Beef Soup with Vermicelli.
Bass, Boiled.
Roast Beef, with potatoes, spinach, and green peas.
Stewed Pigeons.

Dessert.

Cranberry and Rice Jelly.—Strain the berries after boiling, and thicken with ground rice, sweeten, boil gently, and serve with cream.

Snow Cream.—Put to a quart of cream (or milk) the whites of 3 eggs well beaten, 4 spoonfuls sweet wine, sugar to taste, and whip to a froth.

Pine-apple and nuts.

Tea, or Lunch.

Cold quail, roast beef, Anchovy toast, Turk's cap, oyster patties, waffles, rolls, quince jelly, sponge cake.

SUNDAY.

Breakfast.— Omelet, cold tongue, pickled salmon, brown bread, milk toast, broiled tripe, biscuit, bread. Tea and coffee.

Dinner.

Spring Soup.—Strong veal or mutton broth, thickened with greens, asparagus, etc.

Trout.

Roast Ducks, with peas, asparagus, and rice.

Beefsteak, with Mushrooms.

Cold Ham.

Dessert.

Bakewell Pudding.—The yolks of 4 eggs and whites of 2 eggs, with $\frac{1}{2}$ lb. powdered sugar, and $\frac{1}{4}$ clarified butter. When well mixed, stir over the fire, till it thickens. Line a dish with puff paste, and put in a layer of candied peel about an inch thick; then pour the mixture on it, and bake in a slow oven.

Italian Cream.—Juice of a lemon, grated rind of 2, and 1 qt. cream. Stir over the fire till thick.

Chocolate bonbons and nuts.

Tea, or Lunch.

Omelet with parsley, clam fritters, milk toast, pâté de foie gras, cold meat, veal cake, pound cake, preserved cherries. Tea.

JUNE.

MONDAY.

Breakfast.—Fried trout, pickled tongue, potted game, steam toast, Graham biscuit, boiled eggs, cucumbers. Tea and coffee.

DINNER.

Green Pea Soup.—Boil 1 qt. fresh peas in salt water, with a handful of parsley and sorrel, until perfectly tender. Drain, and pound in a mortar, and mix gradually into veal or beef broth. Season with pepper and salt, fry some boiled onions and lettuce, with bread cut into dice, and put into the soup before serving, also a few heads of boiled asparagus.

Boiled Salmon, melted butter.

Broiled Chicken, with peas, string beans, and potatoes.

Fricandels of Veal.—Chop the fat and lean of 3 lbs. of a loin of veal very fine; then soak a French roll in some milk; beat 3 eggs; add pepper, salt, and mace. Make the mixture somewhat in the shape of a small chicken, rub it with egg and bread-crumbs, fry until brown, pour off the fat, boil water in the pan, and stew the fricandels in this gravy; two will make a handsome dish; thicken the gravy.

Dessert.

Macaroni Pudding.—Simmer 1 or 2 oz. of pipe macaroni in a pint of milk, with a bit of lemon and cinnamon, till tender; put it into a dish with milk, 2 or 3 yolks of eggs, but only 1 white; sugar, nutmeg, a spoonful of peach water, and ½ glass raisin wine. Bake with paste around the edges.

Bohemian Cream.—Rub a pint of fresh strawberries through a sieve, add 6 oz. powdered sugar, the juice of a lemon, 1½ oz. isinglass dissolved in ½ pt. water. Mix all together, and set on the ice, stirring till it begins to set. Whip a pint of cream to a froth, and stir into the strawberries, letting the mould remain on ice till wanted. Then put it into warm water for an instant, and turn out.

Cherries and nuts.

Tea, or Lunch.

Radishes, cucumbers, cold veal, potted fish, broiled smoked salmon, muffins, rolls, sponge cake, strawberries. Tea.

TUESDAY.

Breakfast.— Cold birds, omelet, minced salt fish, cream toast, radishes, water-cresses, rolls, tea and coffee, strawberries.

Dinner.

Gumbo Soup.
Trout.
Roast Veal, with asparagus, lettuce, peas, and potatoes.

Pigeons, with Peas.—Put the pigeons into a stewpan with a little butter, just to stiffen; then take them out, put some small slices of bacon into the pan, give a fine color, draw them, and add a spoonful of flour to the butter; then put in the pigeons and bacon, moisten by degrees with gravy, and bring it to the consistency of sauce; boil it; season with parsley, young onions, and let it simmer; when half done put in a quart of peas; shake them often; and when ready thicken the peas with flour and butter. There should be no gravy left.

Dessert.

Quaking Pudding.—Scald 1 qt. cream (or milk); and when almost cold add 4 eggs well beaten, 1½ spoonfuls flour, some nutmeg, and sugar; tie it close in a buttered cloth; boil 1 hour, and serve with wine sauce.

Crème au Marasquin.—Whip a pint of cream until it thickens, add powdered sugar, a glass of maraschino, and 1 oz. isinglass dissolved in water. The latter must be liquid, but cold.

Strawberries and cream, nuts.

TEA, OR LUNCH.

Cold boiled ham, cucumbers, dried beef with cream, biscuit, rolls, strawberries, bread, cake. Tea and chocolate.

WEDNESDAY.

Breakfast.—Minced veal, pickled shad roes, potted game, corn muffins, dry toast, radishes, rolls, scrambled eggs. Tea and coffee.

DINNER.

Mutton Broth.

Baked Pike, caper sauce.

Mutton Pillan, with peas, beans, and potatoes. Take ½ lb. neck of mutton, boil it well, then cut it into small pieces, and fry it in butter; then let it simmer ½ an hour with 2 cups boiled rice, a few cloves, a little cinnamon, and some cardamoms.

Squabs, roasted.

Dessert.

Plum Pudding, not rich.—Four oz. each of grated bread, suet, and stoned raisins, mix with 2 well-beaten eggs, 4 spoonfuls of milk, and a little salt. Boil 4 hours. A spoonful of brandy, sugar, and nutmeg, in melted butter, may be used as sauce.

Raspberry Cream.—Boil 1 oz. isinglass in 1½ pts. milk; strain through a hair sieve; boil 1½ pts. cream; when cool add ½ pt. raspberry juice to it; then add the milk, stir well, sweeten, and add a glass of brandy. Whisk it till nearly cold, then put in a mould.

Strawberries and nuts.

TEA, OR LUNCH.

Cold tongue, miroton of veal, cucumbers, radishes, strawberries, pound cake, waffles, toast, rolls, tea and chocolate.

THURSDAY.

Breakfast.—Boiled chicken, clam fritters, muffins, steam toast, hot brown bread, cucumbers, strawberries, tea and coffee, boiled eggs.

Dinner.

Tomato Soup.

Lobster.

Roast Beef, with peas, lima beans, and potatoes.

Rissoles.—Pound cold meat, season, and mix with a little good gravy and butter. Roll paste into oval pieces, lay a spoonful on one end, double it over, press the edges together, and scallop them. Brush over with yolk of egg, and fry brown.

Dessert.

Cherry Pie.

Orange Butter.—Boil 6 eggs hard, beat them in a mortar with 2 oz. fine sugar, 3 oz. butter, and 2 oz. blanched almonds, beaten to a paste; moisten with orange-flower water, and when all is mixed rub it through a colander on a dish. Serve with sweet biscuits.

Strawberries, pine-apple, and nuts.

Tea, or Lunch.

Potted shrimps, dried chipped beef, milk toast, rolls, corn pone, strawberries, radishes, chocolate.

FRIDAY.

Breakfast.—Cold roast beef, smelts, omelet, chipped potatoes, rice cakes, Graham bread, water cresses, radishes, cucumbers, tea and coffee.

Dinner.

Soup à la Bisque.
Fresh Mackerel.

Roast Lamb, with peas, asparagus, tomatoes, and lettuce.

Sweetbreads.

Lobster Pie.—Cut 2 boiled lobsters in pieces, and lay in a dish; beat the spawn in a mortar; put the shells on to boil in some water, with 3 spoonfuls of vinegar, pepper, salt, and some mace. A large piece of butter rolled in flour must be added when the good is obtained. Pour into the dish strained, strew in some crumbs, and put a paste over all. Bake only till the paste is done.

Dessert.

Rhubarb Pie.

Lemon Syllabub.—Grate the peel of a lemon with *lump sugar*, and dissolve the sugar in ¾ pt. of wine; add the juice of half a lemon, and ¼ pt. cream. Whisk the whole until properly thick, and put into glasses.

Strawberries, cherries, and bonbons.

Tea, or Lunch.

Kidney Toast.—(Take cold veal kidneys, cut in small pieces; pound the fat in a mortar, with salt, pepper, and a boiled onion. Bind all together with beaten whites of eggs, heap it on toast, cover with yolks beaten, sprinkle with bread crumbs, and bake in the oven.) Salt fish broiled, cold ham, raised biscuit, corn-bread, fruit, cucumbers, and radishes. Lemon cheese-cakes.—(Mix 4 oz. sifted lump sugar, with 4 oz. butter; then add yolks of 2 and white of 1 egg, the rind of 3 lemons chopped fine and the juice of $1\frac{1}{2}$, 1 Savoy biscuit, some blanched almonds, and 3 spoonfuls of brandy. Bake in patty pans.) Tea and cocoa.

SATURDAY.

Breakfast.—Broiled fresh salmon, beefsteak, fried potatoes, cream toast, Graham biscuit, potted tongue, rolls, tea and coffee.

DINNER.

Bean Soup.

Soles, fried.

Boiled Leg of Mutton, with lettuce, peas, spinach, and potatoes.

Beefsteaks, with mushrooms.

Chicken Patties.

Dessert.

Sweetmeat Pudding.—Cover a dish with thin puff paste, and lay in it 1 oz. each of candied lemon, orange, and citron, sliced thin. Beat the yolks of 8 and whites of 2 eggs, and mix with 8 oz. butter warmed, and some white sugar. Pour all over the sweetmeats, and bake 1 hour in a moderate oven.

Flemish Cream.—Dissolve $\frac{1}{2}$ oz. isinglass in 1 pt. water, strain it to $\frac{1}{4}$ pt. cream; add 1 glass brandy, and whisk to a light froth. Put in a mould.

Cherries and candied fruits.

Tea, or Lunch.

Cold lamb, sandwiches of ham, sardines, waffles, dry toast, rolls, cucumbers, strawberries, small pound-cakes, tea.

SUNDAY.

Breakfast.—Broiled kidneys, with tomato sauce, cold veal, scrambled eggs, Graham bread, gems, rolls, bread, tea and coffee, radishes.

Dinner.

Asparagus Soup.—To 2 qts. of good beef or veal broth, put 4 onions, 2 turnips, and some sweet herbs, with the white parts of a hundred young asparagus. If large, half the quantity will do. Let them simmer till tender enough to rub through a tammy, then strain and season, adding boiled tops of asparagus.

Boiled Salmon.

Chickens à la Carmelite, with peas, beans, and potatoes. Put a piece of butter, size of a walnut, in a stew-pan; as it melts dredge in flour, and when well mixed add a teacup of milk. Cut up the chickens and add them, with pepper, an onion, and mace. Stew till tender, adding milk and water, if too dry. Take out the chickens, and cover with chopped parsley and lemon-juice mixed; thicken the sauce, and add a glass of white-wine.

Beefsteak, broiled.

Dessert.

Mother Eve's Pudding.—Grate ¾ lb. bread; mix with same quantity chopped suet, the same of apples and currants; mix with these 4 eggs, and the rind of half a lemon shred fine. Boil in a shape 3 hours, and serve with sauce.

French Flummery.—Boil slowly 2 oz. isinglass shavings in a quart of cream, 15 minutes. Stir, and sweeten with loaf sugar; add a spoonful of rose-water, and one of orange-flower water. Strain into a form.

Cherries, strawberries, and nuts.

Tea, or Lunch.

Ham cake, cold corned beef, minced salt fish, crackers and cheese, toast, corn bannock, biscuit, macaroons, strawberries, cucumbers, tea.

JULY.

MONDAY.

Breakfast.—Sweetbreads fried, potted fish, raw tomatoes sliced, fried potatoes, cucumbers, cream toast, rolls, water-cresses. Tea and coffee.

Dinner.

Vegetable Soup.—Veal or beef broth, with all sorts of vegetables cut small.

Boiled Codfish, with sauce.

Boiled Chickens.—With tomatoes, potatoes roasted, peas, and green corn.

Beefsteak Pudding.—Take 1½ lb. of the inside of a sirloin, beat it tender, cut thin, and divide into small slices, with 2 kidneys. Season with pepper, salt, and chopped parsley, roll in paste, and boil 3 hours. When done, have ready strong beef-gravy, with mushroom ketchup in it, make a hole in the paste, and pour it into the pudding.

Dessert.

Cherry Pudding.

Delicate dish.—Beat whites of eggs with currant jelly, to a solid froth, and serve with cream and sugar.

Raspberries, cherries, and nuts.

Tea, or Lunch.

Cold tongue, sardines, veal cake, cucumbers, raspberries, muffins, toast, bread, cake, cherries. Tea.

TUESDAY.

Breakfast.—Spring chickens, fried, with cream sauce; dry toast, rice cakes, raw tomatoes dressed, cold corned beef, cucumbers, fruit, tea and coffee, rolls.

Dinner.

Tomato Soup.—Beef soup with tomatoes pulped or shredded, and well seasoned.

Salmon, boiled.

Fillet of Veal, stuffed, with beans, tomatoes, and potato loaves. Mash the potatoes without milk, make them into conical loaves with butter to hold them, and brown under the meat.

Rice Croquettes.—Boil 6 oz. rice in broth, let it stew till done, then work it well with a spoonful of white sauce, 2 of grated cheese, and a little pepper. When of proper consistence, make the rice into shapes, hollowing them in the hand like cups; then fill them with any kind of minced meat, close the end to contain it, and cover well with the following mixture: 2 spoonfuls grated cheese, with 4 of bread crumbs, stuck together with yolks of eggs; fry a light brown.

Dessert.

Raspberry Pie.
Soft Boiled Custard.
Cherries, and bonbons.

Tea, or Lunch.

Cold chicken pie, broiled smoked salmon, raspberries and cherries, waffles, corn bread, bread, cucumbers, fruit-cake.

WEDNESDAY.

Breakfast.—Lamb cutlet breaded, cold ham, omelet with parsley, steam toast, rolls, bread, corn pone, cucumbers, and fruit.

Dinner.

Green Corn Soup.—Veal broth with 2 ears of green corn grated into it.

Bluefish Broiled.

Roast Chickens, with corn, beans, peas, and potato omelet. Mashed potato, mixed with 4 eggs, well seasoned, and fried.

Calves' Brains.—Cut prepared brains into slices $\frac{1}{2}$ an inch thick; flour, egg, and bread-crumb them; fry a nice brown, and serve with tomato sauce.

Dessert.

Gooseberry Pudding. — Stew gooseberries till they will pulp, then press a pint of the juice through a coarse sieve, and beat it with 3 eggs well beaten, 1½ oz. butter, and enough sugar to sweeten it. Add a few bread-crumbs, and bake in dish with a crust round it.

Almond Custard.—Boil 2 or 3 bitter almonds in a pint of milk or cream, with a stick of cinnamon, a piece of lemon peel, and 8 lumps of sugar; let it simmer; then strain it, and stir till cold. Add the yolks of 6 eggs beaten, 1 oz. of sweet almonds beaten fine in rose water, and stir over the fire till of a proper thickness. Do not boil. Raspberries, cherries, and chocolate caramels.

TEA, OR LUNCH.

Broiled ham, dried beef chipped, biscuit, crackers and cheese, cucumbers stewed. (Peel and slice thick, stew with salt and pepper, and simmer slowly in a little broth or butter; add a little flour before serving.) Raspberries, sponge cake, anchovy, toast. Tea and chocolate.

THURSDAY.

Breakfast.—Minced salmon with cream, cold chicken, corn muffins, rolls, toast, cucumbers, and fruit. Tea and coffee.

Dinner.

Summer Soup.—Take 2 cucumbers, 12 onions, 3 potatoes, 1 lettuce, and a head of white cabbage; fry together in butter; then stew 3 hours in 3 pts. stock; add a little mint, parsley, and a pint of green peas; let it stew 2 hours more; press it through a seive, and thicken with butter and flour.

Trout.

Roast Lamb, mint sauce, with corn, peas, potatoes stewed, and maccaroni with cheese.

Chicken Pudding. — Fricassee 2 young chickens, season with mushroom powder, mace, and salt. Make gravy of the giblets and a bit of meat, put 2 spoonfuls into the paste. Boil 2 hours, and put the rest of the gravy into or under the pudding.

Dessert.

Rice Custards, Strawberry Jelly. — Boil ¾ lb. loaf sugar in a pint of water 20 minutes, pour hot over a quart of picked strawberries, and let them stand over night. Clarify 2½ oz. isinglass in a pint of water, drain the syrup from the berries, adding the juice of a lemon. When the isinglass is nearly cold mix all together, add more sugar if wanted, and put it into moulds. Set on the ice.

Raspberries and almonds.

Tea, or Lunch.

Potted fish, broiled kidneys, minced salt fish, *Vegetable Ragout.* (Cut any kinds of cold vegetables into slices, put in a stewpan with pepper, salt, a little broth, and a piece of butter, and stir till quite hot). Cucumbers and fruit, corn pone, rolls, toast. *Coffee Cakes.* (1 lb. flour. $\frac{1}{4}$ lb. butter, do. sugar, 1 egg, 1 oz. caraway seeds; mix with warm milk and a spoonful rose water; roll out thin, and bake on little tins.) Tea and chocolate.

FRIDAY.

Breakfast.—Broiled beefsteak, trout, stewed potatoes, pickled salmon, hot brown bread, rolls, tea and coffee, *Kedgeree.*—Boil 2 tablespoonfuls of rice, add any fish previously cooked (salmon preferable), nicely picked; beat up an egg well, and stir it in just before serving.

Dinner.

Macaroni Soup.
Flounders.
Fillet of Beef, with corn, peas, beans, and tomatoes.
Corned Beef.

Dessert.

Almond Pudding.—Take $2\frac{1}{2}$ oz. bread crumbs, and steep them in a pint of cream, (or milk), then pound $\frac{1}{2}$

pint of blanched almonds to a paste, with some water, beat the yolks of 6 eggs, and whites of 3; mix all together, and add 3 oz. sugar, and 1 of beaten butter. Thicken over the fire, and bake in a puff paste.

Blancmange.

Raspberries, cherries, and nuts.

TEA, OR LUNCH.

Cold lamb, sardines, omelet, fried bacon, pâté de foie gras, waffles, toast, berries, cucumbers, pound cake, chocolate.

SATURDAY.

Breakfast.—Veal cutlets, potted game, dropped eggs on toast, steamed toast, broiled ham, rolls, tea and coffee, fruit.

DINNER.

Rice Soup.—Take white stock, season it, and use 1½ lbs. of rice to 2 qts. of broth.

Soles.

Boiled Mutton, caper sauce, with roasted potatoes, peas, and corn.

Chicken Patties.

Dessert.

Lemon Jelly.—Clarify 1½ oz. isinglass in a pint of water; add ½ lb. loaf sugar, and the rind of 2 lemons, cut thin. Strain the juice of 4 lemons, and stir into the cool sugar and isinglass. Take out the peel, and pour into forms.

Berry Pie.

Fruit and nuts.

TEA, OR LUNCH.

Cold corned beef, broiled mackerel, toasted cheese, muffins, toast, rolls, berries, Harrison cake, tea.

SUNDAY.

Breakfast.—Codfish balls, broiled fresh salmon, boiled eggs, gems, fruit, rolls, bread, tea and coffee.

DINNER.

Chicken Broth.

Salmon.

Roast Beef, with potatoes, peas, tomatoes, and beans.

Sweetbreads, fried.

Dessert.

Arrowroot Pudding.

Snow Cream.—Put to a quart of cream the whites of 3 eggs, well beaten, 4 spoonfuls of sweet wine, sugar to taste, and a bit of lemon-peel. Whip to a froth, take out the peel, and serve in a dish.

Early apples, and nuts.

Tea, or Lunch.

Salt fish broiled, cold mutton, cheese, corn bread, Turk's cap, raspberries and cherries, cucumbers, and radishes, toast, ham cake, chocolate cakes, tea.

AUGUST.

MONDAY.

Breakfast.—Broiled halibut, cold tongue, stewed potatoes, raw sliced tomatoes, omelet, rolls, dry toast, cucumbers, fruit, tea and coffee.

Dinner.

Vegetable Marrow Soup.—Boil the marrow and strain, then add to beef or veal broth, thicken with 2 spoonfuls of arrowroot, and a little cream. Do not allow it to boil after the latter is added.

Stewed Codfish.—Cut in slices an inch thick, lay in a large stewpan, and season with salt, pepper, a bunch of herbs, an onion, $\frac{1}{2}$ pt. white-wine, and $\frac{1}{4}$ pt. water. Cover close, and let it simmer five minutes, then squeeze in the juice of a lemon, a piece of butter size of an egg, rolled in flour, and a blade of mace. Let it stew slowly till done, and take out the herbs and onions.

Chicken Pillau, with squash, corn, beans, and potatoes.

Baked Calves' Head.—Wash the head, and place in a large earthen dish, on large iron skewers, laid across the top of the dish; cover it with bread crumbs, grated nutmeg, chopped sweet herbs, a little fine-cut lemon, and flour; thick pieces of butter in the eyes, and all over the head, then flour it again; put in the dish a piece of beef, cut small; herbs, an onion, pepper, mace, cloves, a pint of water, and bake the head a fine brown. Boil the brains with sage, separately. When the head is done enough take it out, and set by the fire to keep warm, then stir all in the dish together, and boil in a stewpan; strain it off, put it in the saucepan again with a piece of butter rolled in flour, the brains and sage chopped fine, a spoonful of catsup, and two spoonfuls of wine. Beat well together, and serve in the dish with the head. Leave the tongue in the head.

Dessert.

Baked Custard.

Whipt Cream.—A qt. cream, the whites of 4 eggs, ½ pt. white-wine, ¼ lb. powdered sugar, 12 drops essence of lemon. Beat to a froth, and put in glasses with a little jelly in the bottom.

Peaches and melons.

Tea, or Lunch.

Cold tongue, minced beef on toast, peaches and cream, cucumbers, corn pone, boiled rice, dry toast, tea, lemonade.

TUESDAY.

Breakfast.—Corned beef hash, cold roast chicken, boiled eggs, steam toast, raised biscuit, lettuce, huckleberries, rolls, coffee and tea.

Dinner.

Giblet Soup.

Baked Pike.—Stuff the pike with grated bread, 2 hard boiled eggs chopped fine, a little nutmeg, lemon peel, and the roe or liver chopped; then lay it in the dish, with the tail in the mouth; put pieces of butter all over it, and sprinkle with flour. Garnish with toast and lemon, and serve with melted butter.

Boiled Corned Beef, with corn, squash, beans, and baked potatoes.

Duck, with Peas.—Put the duck in a deep stewpan, with a piece of butter, (singe it first,) flour it, and turn it two or three times, then pour out all the fat. Put to the duck a pint of good gravy, do. peas, 2 lettuces cut small, sweet herbs, pepper and salt; cover close and stew half an hour. When well done thicken with a little butter and flour, shake all together three or four minutes, and serve in a dish, the duck with the sauce poured over it.

Dessert.

Cream Pudding.—Boil 1 qt. of cream with a blade of mace, and half a nutmeg, grated; let it cool; beat the yolks of 8 eggs, and whites of 3, and mix them with a spoonful of flour, $\frac{1}{4}$ lb. blanched almonds, beaten with rose-water, and by degrees mix in the cream. Tie in a thick cloth well floured, boil half an hour, and when done throw fine sugar and melted butter over it.

Peaches and Cream.

Melons, plums, and bonbons.

TEA, OR LUNCH.

Broiled smoked salmon, lobster salad, corn pone, Graham biscuit, blackberries, peaches and cream, macaroons, and small sponge cakes, dry toast, tea and chocolate.

WEDNESDAY.

Breakfast.—Broiled spring chicken, brown bread, cream toast, cold ham, potted fish, rolls, scrambled eggs, blackberries, cucumbers, tea and coffee.

Dinner.

Codling Soup.—Take the meat from a young cod, pound it in a mortar, with some shred parsley, and bread crumbs soaked in milk; make the mixture up into balls with an egg, seasoned well. Stew down 2 or 3 codlings or haddocks into broth, strain it, pulp the meat through a sieve, boil it with parsley roots, thicken, and serve with the forcemeat balls.

Broiled Bluefish.

Roast Beef, with corn, egg plant, squash, and rice.

Pigeon Fricassée.—Cut 8 pigeons into small pieces, and put in a stewpan with 1 pt. water and same of claret. Season with salt, pepper, mace, an onion, a bunch of herbs, a piece of butter rolled in flour; cover close, and let them stew till there is just enough for sauce; then take out the onion and herbs, beat up the yolks of 3 eggs, push the meat to one side, and stir them into the gravy. Keep stirring till sauce is thick, then put the meat in a dish, and pour over it.

Dessert.

Charlotte Russe.

Ice Cream.—Newport receipt.—1 qt. new milk, with cream to suit, 2 tablespoonfuls cornstarch, yolk of 1 egg, sugar, and flavoring to taste. Wet the starch in a little of the milk, mix with the egg, and stir into the milk boiling hot. When cool, it is ready for the freezer.

Peaches, plums, and hot-house grapes.

Tea, or Lunch.

Cold veal, sardines, Boston crackers, with tomato catsup, cream toast, rice cakes, blackberries and huckleberries, pound-cake, rolls, gems. Tea.

THURSDAY.

Breakfast.—Cold roast beef, sweetbreads fried, raw tomatoes, muffins, potted tongue, rolls and bread, berries, cucumbers. Tea and coffee.

Dinner.

Green Corn Soup.

Baked Cod's Head.—Lay the head in a buttered pan, with a bundle of herbs, an onion stuck with cloves, 3 or 4 blades of mace, $\frac{1}{2}$ spoonful black pepper, a small piece lemon-peel, a bruised nutmeg, a small bit of horseradish, and a quart of water. Flour the head, and stick butter and bread crumbs over it. Bake it well, and lay it in the dish it is to be served in, covered close, and placed over hot water. Boil the liquor 3 or 4 minutes, strain it, and add a gill of wine, 2 spoonfuls of catsup, 1 of mushrooms pickled, and $\frac{1}{4}$ lb. butter rolled in flour. Stir till it is thick, and pour into the dish. Stick pieces of fried bread round the dish, and in the head.

Boiled Lamb, with baked tomatoes, corn, lima beans, and potatoes.

Brown Fricassée.—Cut chickens in small pieces, and rub with yolks of eggs; then roll them in grated bread and nutmeg, and fry a fine brown with butter. Pour off the butter, and add ½ pt. brown gravy, 1 glass white wine, a few mushrooms, salt and pepper, and a little butter rolled in flour. When thick, dish it for the table.

Dessert.

Blackberry Pudding.—A good batter mixed with the fruit, boiled 1 hour, and served with wine sauce.

Kisses.—Beat the whites of 4 eggs till stiff, then stir in gradually (one spoonful at a time) 1 lb. powdered sugar, and add 12 drops essence of lemon. Lay a wet sheet of paper on a square pan, and drop at equal distances a teaspoonful of stiff currant jelly with a little sugar and egg *under* each one. Then pile the froth so as to cover each lump of jelly, as round as possible. Set in a cool oven, and when colored they are done. Place the two bottoms together, lay them lightly on a sieve, and dry in a cool oven till they stick together.

Apples, peaches, and melons.

Tea, or Lunch.

Cold miroton of veal, dried beef stewed in cream, waffles, crackers and cheese, bread and toast, berries and radishes, Indian pound-cake. Tea and chocolate.

FRIDAY.

Breakfast. — Codfish fried, chipped potatoes, cold tongue, minced lamb, omelet, corn bread, brown bread, berries, rolls. Tea and coffee.

DINNER.

Lobster Soup.—Make a stock of small fish, take the meat from 1 or 2 lobsters, and cut in small pieces; lay it aside, and break the shell, boiling it gently several hours with the stock. Make the coral into forcemeat balls, with a small piece of stock fish, bread crumbs, parsley, and egg. When the stock is done, strain, and thicken with butter and flour. Warm the lobster in it, and serve with the balls. It may be seasoned delicately with any sauce.

Boiled Soles, melted butter.

Roast Veal, with peas, beans, and potatoes à la maître d'hôtel.

Neat's Tongue Fricassée.—Boil the tongues till tender, peel, and cut in thin slices; fry them in fresh butter; then pour it out, add enough gravy for sauce, herbs, an onion, pepper, salt, mace, and a glass of white-wine; simmer all $\frac{1}{2}$ an hour; take out the tongue, and strain the gravy; then put both into the pan again with yolks of 2 eggs beaten, a piece of butter size of a walnut, rolled in flour, and a little nutmeg. Shake together 5 minutes, and serve.

Dessert.

Huckleberry Pie.

Apple Soufflé. — Scald and sweeten the fruit, beat through a sieve, and put in a dish. Pour a rich custard 2 inches deep over it; when cold, whip the whites of the eggs to a froth, and lay in rough pieces on the custard; sift fine sugar over it, and put in a slack oven for a short time.

Peaches and melons.

TEA, OR LUNCH.

Ham sandwiches, salad, tongue, potted game, corn muffins, biscuit, jelly tarts, berries, cup cake. Tea.

SATURDAY.

Breakfast. — Beefsteak, cold snipe, raw tomatoes, dropped eggs on toast, milk toast, berries, cucumbers, tea and coffee, rolls.

DINNER.

Oxcheek Soup. — Take the meat from half an ox-head, and put in a pan with 3 sliced, fried onions, herbs, allspice, pepper, and salt, a large spoonful each. Lay the bones close on the meat, and put 1 qt. water to every pound cut meat. Cover the pan with coarse brown paper, tied closely, and let it stand in the oven 4 hours. When done, take out the bones, and pour the soup and meat into a pan. When it is to be used, take off the fat, warm the soup, and cut the meat into pieces not larger than a mouthful. Make the brains into forcemeat balls, and season highly with walnut catsup and cayenne.

Stewed Terrapin.—Boil them 10 minutes, and then take them out, remove the outer shells, and put back again. Then boil till the claws are tender. Take them out of the inner shell, taking care not to break the gall, which must be separated from the liver and thrown away; also the spongy part. Cut them in small pieces, put in a stewpan with salt, pepper, and some butter. After they have stewed a few minutes, put in a wine-glass of water to each terrapin. When they have stewed 10 minutes add butter rolled in flour, and 1 glass white-wine to each one. Stew 5 minutes more, and take off. Add beaten yolks of eggs (1 yolk to 2 terrapins) well stirred in, cover tightly, let it stand 5 minutes, and serve in a deep dish.

Lamb Chops, breaded; with succotash (corn and beans), squash, and potatoes.

Lamb's Head, stewed.—Wash, and lay in water 1 hour; take out the brains, and with a sharp penknife take out the tongue and bones, so as to leave the meat whole; chop together 2 lbs. veal, 2 lbs. beef-suet, thyme, lemon peel; nutmeg grated, 2 rolls grated and yolks of 4 eggs. Tie the head with thread, and stew 2 hours in 2 qts. gravy. Make the mixture into balls, and fry in dripping; beat the brains with parsley, and fry in little cakes; strain the gravy, and season with catsup, and serve the head with the fried balls and brains around it.

Dessert.

Soft Boiled Custard, frozen; with sliced peaches, curds, and whey.—Wash very clean in cold water a piece of rennet 2 inches square; wipe it dry, and pour on it lukewarm water enough to cover it. Let it stand all night, then take it out, and stir the water into a quart of warm milk. Set the milk in a warm place till it becomes a firm curd —then on the ice. Eat with wine, sugar, and nutmeg.

Melons, plums, and nuts.

Tea, or Lunch.

Ham cake, cold beef, sardines, pâté de foie gras, wine jelly, sponge cake, berries, steamed toast, rolls, Indian bannock. Tea.

SUNDAY.

Breakfast.—Broiled salmon, cold corned beef, mutton chops, raw tomatoes, gems, rolls, bread, berries, Indian griddle-cakes.

Dinner.

Tomato Soup.—Chicken or veal broth thickened, with tomato pulp in it.

Perch.

Broiled Quail, with egg-plant, squash, corn, and tomatoes.

Ragout of Veal.—Cut a neck of veal into steaks, flatten with a rolling-pin, season with salt, pepper, and spice, lard them with bacon, lemon-peel, thyme, and dip them in yolks of eggs. Put in a pan with ½ pt. strong gravy, and stew leisurely; season high, and add mushrooms and pickles, also add a glass of wine.

Dessert.

Blackberry Pie.

Lemon Pudding.—Grate the rind of a fresh lemon, and squeeze in the juice. Stir together ¼ lb. powdered sugar, and ¼ lb. butter to a cream; beat 3 eggs well and add; mix all together with a tablespoonful of wine and brandy, and a teaspoonful of rose-water; beat all very hard. Make a paste of 5 oz. flour, and ¼ lb. butter; cover a buttered soup-plate, put in the pudding, and bake a light brown.

Peaches and grapes.

Tea, or Lunch.

Boiled ham, cold birds, crackers, raw tomatoes, waffles, dry toast, biscuit, peaches and cream, berries, German cake—from a Hungarian Countess (1 lb. sugar, 1 lb. beaten almonds, 1 lb. citron beaten, 1 oz. mace, cinnamon and cloves mixed. Make as stiff as pie-crust, roll out an inch thick, cut in shapes, and glaze with sugar and water. It will keep a year.) Tea and chocolate.

SEPTEMBER.

MONDAY.

Breakfast.—Cold chicken pie, broiled ham, scrambled eggs, fried potatoes, rolls, cream toast, berries and peaches, tea and coffee.

DINNER.

Soup à la Creci.—Grate the red part of 12 carrots, slice 4 onions, a turnip, 2 lettuces, a piece of lean ham, a few sprigs of parsley and thyme, and a few allspice; put them all in a stewpan with a piece of butter; let it simmer $\frac{1}{2}$ an hour, then fill up with stock, and allow it to boil gently 2 hours; put in the crumb of 2 rolls, and rub the whole through a tamis. Let it boil, skim it, add salt to taste, and a small lump of sugar. Put a little boiled rice in the tureen.

Cutlets of Sole.—Cut the sole in pieces crosswise, dry flour, egg, and crumb them; fry crisp, and dish with parsley in the centre.

Green Goose Roasted, with roast potatoes, squash, corn and tomatoes.

Stewed Beef.—Stew the brisket in water enough to cover it; when tender take out the bones, and skim the fat; strain the gravy, and add a glass of wine and a small muslin bag of spice; have ready boiled vegetables, with mushrooms, cut them in shapes, and lay around and upon the beef. Pour the gravy over it.

Dessert.

Bread-and-butter Pudding.—Make a custard of 1 egg, and ½ pt. milk, by boiling the milk with lemon peel, and sugar, putting it on the fire with the egg to thicken; butter slices of bread or roll, and soak them an hour or two in the custard, then lay them in a dish with currants, and powdered sugar between each layer. Then pour over it another ½ pt. milk beaten with 2 eggs, and bake.

Crème au caramel.

Peaches and pears.

Tea, or Lunch.

Cold mutton, tongue, Turk's cap, muffins, potted fish, cracker milk toast, jelly cake, berries, peaches, dry toast, tea.

TUESDAY.

Breakfast.—Beef hash, pickled tripe, stewed potatoes, corn bannock, rolls, bread, raw tomatoes, berries, and fruit.

Dinner.

Potato Soup.

Bluefish.

Roast Lamb, with beans, tomatoes, potatoes, and corn fritters. Grate corn into a batter, and fry on a griddle.

Beef's Heart Roasted.

Dessert.

Baked Batter Pudding.—Make a batter with 6 oz. flour, 1 gill milk and 4 eggs; make it the consistency of cream with more milk, and bake in cups. Cold sauce.

Almond Croquantes.—Blanch and dry 1 lb. almonds, pound in a mortar with 1 lb. powdered sugar, rub through a wire sieve, then rub in $\frac{3}{4}$ lb. butter, grated rind $\frac{1}{2}$ a lemon, and yolks 3 eggs. Make into a paste, cut in shapes, and bake in a quick oven. When done dip them in sugar boiled to a syrup.

Pears, plums, and grapes.

Tea, or Lunch.

Cold goose, dried beef chipped, waffles, raw tomatoes, steam toast, berries, breadcake. Tea.

WEDNESDAY.

Breakfast.—Broiled kidneys, cold lamb, stewed tomatoes, boiled eggs, Graham biscuit, rolls, milk toast, baked potatoes. Tea and coffee.

Dinner.

Beef Soup.

Roast Lobster.—Remove the shells from boiled lobsters, lay them before the fire, and baste them with butter till they have a fine froth. Dish them with plain melted butter.

Bouilli, with corn, beans, egg-plant, and potatoes. Take from 4 to 6 lbs. of rump of beef, and allow 1 pt. cold water to every pound of meat; let it *simmer gently* four or five hours, with a bunch of herbs, and an onion stuck with cloves; then strain off the soup, leaving enough for sauce, to be served with the meat. Season with catsup, thicken, and add vegetables cut in shapes.

Boned Lamb.—Bone the shoulder, stuff it with fine force-meat, and skewer it in a nice shape. Put it in a closely covered stewpan with 2 oz. butter, and a teacup of water, until the gravy is drawn; cut the brisket in pieces, and stew them in gravy thickened with milk and egg; thicken the gravy of the shoulder with any vegetables in season. Place the shoulder in a dish with its gravy, and lay the brisket with white sauce around it.

Dessert.

Blackberry Pie.

Peach Pudding.—Scald till soft 12 peaches; put grated bread into a pint of boiling milk, and when half cold add 4 oz. sugar, the yolks of 4 eggs beaten, and 1 glass of white wine. Mix with the pulp of the fruit, and bake in a paste.

Pears and grapes.

TEA, OR LUNCH.

Sardines, broiled ham, cold chicken, crackers and cheese, corn bread, buttered toast, berries, Harrison cake. Tea.

THURSDAY.

Breakfast.—Liver hash, stewed mushrooms, cold ham, corn pone, raw tomatoes, cucumbers, fruit, fried potatoes, griddle-cakes, rolls. Tea and coffee.

DINNER.

Green Corn Soup.

Blackfish.

Roast Chickens, with beans, baked tomatoes, and potatoes.

Cold Tongue.

Dessert.

Huckleberry Pudding.—Put $\frac{1}{2}$ lb. flour into a pan with a little salt, and add gently $\frac{1}{2}$ pt. milk. Beat the whites of 4 eggs to a solid froth, and add just as the batter is to be used. Make it of a proper consistency with milk, and stir in the fruit. It may be baked or boiled.

Custard Cream of Chocolate.

Peaches, plums, and grapes.

Tea, or Lunch.

Cold boned lamb, lobster salad, muffins, toast, gingerbread, berries and peaches, sponge cake, crackers and cheese. Tea and chocolate.

FRIDAY.

Breakfast.—Broiled whitefish, cold tongue, dropped eggs, chipped potatoes, sliced onions and cucumbers, milk toast, rolls, berries.

Dinner.

Eel Soup.—Skin 3 lbs. small eels; bone 1 or 2, cut in little pieces, and fry lightly with a bit of butter, and parsley. Put to the remainder 3 qts. water, a crust of bread, 3 blades mace, an onion, some whole pepper, and a bunch of herbs. Cover, and stew till the fish breaks from the bones; then strain it off, pound to a paste, and pass through a sieve. Cut some toasted bread into dice, pour the soup on it, add the scallops of eel, and serve: ¼ pt. cream or milk with a teaspoonful of flour rubbed smooth in it, is a great improvement.

Baked Codfish.

Leg of Mutton, stuffed; with corn, squash, and potatoes.

Stewed Larks.

Dessert.

Rolypoly Pudding.—Make a rich paste of butter and flour, as light as possible. Roll it thin, 8 or 10 inches wide, and as long as you please; then spread a thick layer of fruit or jam upon it, leaving an inch of the edges bare. Then roll it round, lapping it over to secure the fruit. Wrap in a floured cloth, and boil 2 or 3 hours.

Imperial Cream.

Melons and pears.

Tea, or Lunch.

Cold pigeon pie, pickled herring, baked potatoes, rusk, steam toast, berries and fruit, crackers and cheese, tarts. Tea and chocolate.

SATURDAY.

Breakfast.—Codfish balls, stewed eels, potted game, potatoes à la maître d'hôtel, rolls, brown bread, fruit. Tea and coffee.

Dinner.

Soupe à la Julienne.

Haddock, boiled.

Roast Veal, with corn, limas beans, squash, and potatoes.

Pilau of Rabbit.—Cut up the rabbit; pound an onion in mortar, extract the juice, and mix it with a saltspoon of ground ginger, a teaspoonful of salt, and the juice of a lemon. Rub this into the meat; cut up 2 onions in slices, and fry them in ¼ lb. butter; when brown take them out, put in the rabbit, and let them stew together. Have ½ lb. rice half boiled in broth; put the meat and all into a jar, with ½ pint milk, whole pepper, ¼ doz. cloves, and a little salt. Secure the mouth, and bake until done, adding a little broth to moisten if necessary.

Dessert.

Huckleberry Pudding.

Calf's-foot Jelly.—Boil a cow-heel in 2 qts. of water for 7 or 8 hours: take every particle of fat and sediment from the jelly; when cold put to it a pint of wine, the juice of 3 lemons, and rind of 2 pared thin, 6 oz. sugar, the whites and shells of 3 eggs well beaten, and ½ oz. insinglass. Boil 20 minutes, and after adding a teacup of cold water, boil 5 minutes more; then cover close, and let it stand ½ an hour to cool; pour through a jelly-bag till clear, and put in a mould on the ice.

Melons, pears, and plums.

TEA, OR LUNCH.

Cold beef, with tomato catsup, salad, potted fish, tongue, corn muffins, dry toast, berries and fruit, cucumbers and radishes, fruit cake. Tea.

SUNDAY.

Breakfast.—Lamb chops, potato cakes, stewed tomatoes, pickled tongue, rolls, gems, berries and fruit. Tea and coffee.

DINNER.

Soup Maigre. — Pare and slice 5 or 6 cucumbers, and add to them the inside of as many lettuces, a sprig of mint, 2 onions, 1½ pts. peas, and a little parsley. Put them into a saucepan with salt and pepper, and ½ lb. butter, to stew gently in their own liquor ½ an hour, then add 2 qts. boiling water, and stew them 2 hours; rub a little flour into a teacup of water, boil 15 or 20 minutes with the rest, and serve it.

Stewed Scallops. — Boil in salt and water (after straining off the liquor), then stew in the liquor, adding butter rolled in flour, cloves, and mace.

Roast Ham, with corn, beans, and tomatoes. Soak

the ham in lukewarm water for a day or two, changing the water often. Roast it slowly before the fire, basting with hot water, and when done dredge it all over with fine bread-crumbs, and brown.

Veal Cutlets, with Rice.—Pound a cupful of rice boiled in milk, with pepper and salt, in a mortar; cold veal in the same way; mix together with yolk of egg, from into cutlets, brush with yolk of egg, and fry them. Cover them with mushrooms pickled, or any piquant sauce.

Dessert.

Soft boiled Custard.

Transparent Pudding.—Beat 8 eggs, put them into a stewpan with ½ lb. powdered sugar, same of butter, and some grated nutmeg. Keep stirring on the fire till it thickens. Put a puff paste round the edge of the dish, pour in the pudding *cool*, and bake in a moderate oven. Add candied orange and citron if you like.

Peaches, melons, and grapes.

TEA, OR LUNCH.

Broiled smoked salmon, cold ham, dried beef, boiled rice, corn bread, toast, berries and fruit, tomatoes dressed, German cake.

OCTOBER.

MONDAY.

Breakfast.—Cold chicken, minced veal on toast, fried scallops, omelet, baked potatoes, corn pone, milk toast, berries. Tea and coffee.

DINNER.

Macaroni Soup.
Halibut.
Roast Woodcock, with squash, egg-plant, tomatoes, and potatoes.
Chicken Pie.

Dessert.

Quince Pudding.
Burnt Cream.
Grapes, pears, and nuts.

TEA, OR LUNCH.

Ham cake, potted game, sardines, waffles, gems, biscuit, stewed pears, Spanish buns, breadcake. Tea and chocolate.

TUESDAY.

Breakfast.—Broiled liver, cold mutton, tomatoes, fried potatoes, cold woodcock, cracker milk toast, rolls. Tea and coffee.

DINNER.

Oyster Soup.
Boiled Codfish.
Roast Beef, with potatoes, cauliflower, and squash.
Miroton of Veal.

Dessert.

Apple Charlotte.—Pare and slice apples; cut slices of bread and butter; place the latter all around the inside of a buttered pie-dish; then put in a layer of apples sprinkled with chopped lemon peel, and considerable brown sugar; then put in a layer of the bread, and one of apples, repeating till the dish is full. Squeeze over all the juice of lemons, so that it will be well flavored. Cover up the dish with crusts, bake $1\frac{1}{4}$ hours, remove the crust, and turn out.

Vanilla Cream.

Pears, grapes, and nuts.

TEA, OR LUNCH.

Cold chicken pie, fried oysters, chopped vegetables on toast, peaches and cream, Graham bread, rolls. Tea and chocolate.

WEDNESDAY.

Breakfast.— Minced beef, cold ham, dropped eggs, chipped potatoes, Indian griddle-cakes, rolls. Tea and coffee.

Dinner.

Pea Soup.
Baked Pike.
Boiled Leg of Mutton, caper sauce, with stewed potatoes, cabbage, beans, and spinach.
Sweetbreads, stewed.

Dessert.

Brandy Pudding.
Peach Pie.
Grapes, apples, and almonds.

Tea, or Lunch.

Clam fritters, potted game, veal sandwiches, apple sauce, muffins, toast, corn bannock, sponge cake. Tea.

THURSDAY.

Breakfast.—Pickle shad roes, broiled oysters, mutton chops, corn bread, milk toast, rolls. Tea and coffee.

Dinner.

Tomato Soup.
Smelts.
Roast Partridges, with squash, egg-plant, and hominy.
Stewed Beef.

Dessert

Arrowroot Pudding.
Baked Custard.
Candied fruits, bonbons, and nuts.

Tea, or Lunch.

Pickled oysters, broiled ham, flour griddle-cakes, with sugar and nutmeg, rice balls, stewed plums, jelly cakes, tea, toast, crackers and cheese.

FRIDAY.

Breakfast.—Broiled halibut, fried scallops, cold boiled chickens, poached eggs, milk toast of brown bread, muffins, rolls. Tea and coffee.

Dinner.

Vermicelli Soup.
Bluefish.
Roast Pork, with apple-sauce, tomatoes, squash, and potatoes.
Scalloped Oysters.

Dessert.

Apple Pie.
Blancmange.
Grapes, pears, and figs.

Tea, or Lunch.

Cold birds, tongue, ham toast, cheese, cream cakes raised biscuit, steam toast, baked sweet apples, fruit cake.

SATURDAY.

Breakfast.—Corned beef hash, cold tongue, potted fish, brown bread, corn pone, rolls. Tea and coffee.

Dinner.

Clam Soup.
Soles.
Boiled Chickens, oyster sauce, with potatoes, egg plant, baked potatoes, and squash.
Boiled Tongue.

Dessert.

Damson Pudding.—Take a few spoonfuls from a qt. of milk, and mix into it by degrees 4 spoonfuls flour, 2 of ginger, and a little salt; then add the rest of the milk, and 1 lb. of damsons. Tie it in a wet, floured cloth, and boil 1½ hour; pour over it melted butter and sugar.

Chocolate Cream.

Grapes, pears, and nuts.

Tea, or Lunch.

Broiled salt mackerel, cold roast pork, raw oysters, baked pears, muffins, doughnuts, fried bread, rolls, cupcake. Tea.

SUNDAY.

Breakfast.—Cold roast duck, fried potatoes, hominy, omelet with parsley, minced fresh fish, brown bread milk toast, corn bannock, rolls. Tea and cocoa.

Dinner.

Veal Broth.
Baked Whitefish.
Roast Veal, with cauliflower, spinach, and potatoes.
Broiled Snipe.

Dessert.

Rice Pudding.
Lemon Cream.
Oranges, apples, and grapes.

Tea, or Lunch.

Chicken patties, potted tongue, sardines, dry toast, crackers and cheese, preserved quinces, Graham biscuit, rolls, macaroons and cocoanut cakes. Tea.

NOVEMBER.

MONDAY.

Breakfast.—Pork steak, cold quail, pickled scallops, baked potatoes, milk tost of brown bread, rolls. Tea and coffee.

DINNER.

Harrico Soup.—Take mutton cutlets, trim, and fry to light brown; then stew in 3 qts. of brown gravy soup till tender. Take 2 carrots, 2 onions, celery cut fine, a glass of port wine, and one of mushroom catsup, and add to the soup, after straining. Cook till all is tender, and thicken with a little butter and flour.

Blackfish, boiled.

Roast Beef, with lima beans, squash, and potatoes.

Spiced Veal.—Two and a half lbs. of veal well chopped, 4 crackers pounded fine, 2 eggs, 2 slices of pork chopped fine, a piece of butter size of an egg, $\frac{1}{2}$ teaspoonful pepper, and same of salt. Put into a shape, cover with bread crumbs, and bake 2 hours.

Dessert.

Carrot Pie.—Boil and strain 6 carrots to a pulp, add 3 pts. milk, 6 eggs, 2 tablespoonfuls butter melted, juice of ½ a lemon, and grated rind of a whole one. Sweeten and bake in a deep dish.

Sponge Pudding.—Butter a mould thickly, and fill it three parts full of small sponge cakes soaked in wine, then fill up the mould with a rich cold custard. Put a buttered paper over the mould, and bake it. Serve with wine sauce.

Plums, pears, and chestnuts.

Tea, or Lunch.

Rice Cakes. (Soak ½ lb. rice over night, boil soft, drain dry, mix ¼ lb. butter with it, and set away to cool. Then stir it into a qt. of milk, stir in ½ pt. flour, and add 6 eggs with salt. Fry thin on a griddle). Cold tongue. *Potted Fish.* (Boil lobsters, shrimps, or any shell-fish, pick out the meat, and put in a stew-pan with a little butter, chopped mushrooms, and a little salt. Simmer gently, then add the yolks of 2 eggs beaten with a cup-full of milk or cream, and a little chopped parsley. Let all stew till of the consistency of paste, then put into a pot, and press down. When cold cover with melted butter, and tie on an oil-skin cover). French rolls, Graham bread, stewed quinces. Tea and coffee.

Cup-cake, with hickory nuts.

TUESDAY.

Breakfast.— Cold turkey, sweetbreads, stewed with mushrooms, buckwheat cakes, wheaten grits with cream, rolls and bread. Coffee.

DINNER.

White Soup.—Take broth made of veal, or white poultry, cut the meat off, and put the bone back, adding 2 or 3 shank-bones of mutton, and $\frac{1}{4}$ lb. fine lean bacon, with a bunch of sweet herbs, a piece of fresh lemon-peel, 2 or 3 onions, 3 blades of mace, and a dessertspoonful of white pepper. Boil all till the meat falls quite to pieces, and strain.

Trout.

Roast Prairie Chickens, with sweet potatoes, rice, and beets, spiced currants.

Hock.—One lb. rump steak, do. pork steak, $\frac{1}{2}$ loaf of bread. Chop together like sausage-meat, add 2 eggs, and season with salt, pepper, and sage. Bake like bread, and cut in slices.

Dessert.

Quaking Pudding.—Scald 1 qt. of cream (or milk), and when almost cold add 4 eggs well beaten, $1\frac{1}{2}$ spoonfuls of flour, nutmeg, and sugar, Tie it close in a buttered cloth, boil one hour, turn it out with care, and serve with wine sauce.

Cranberry Tarts.

Pears and hickory nuts.

TEA, OR LUNCH.

Cold lamb with tomato catsup. *Kidney Fritters.* (4 eggs well beaten, with a teacup of cream or milk, pepper and salt, pounded mace, chopped parsley, and mushrooms, or mushroom catsup. Chop the kidneys fine, and mix together; pour into a buttered pan, and stir over the fire.) Muffins, Graham crackers, bread, quince jelly, macaroons. Tea.

WEDNESDAY.

Breakfast.—Beef hash, salt mackerel broiled, cold duck, buckwheat cakes, rolls, boiled hominy. Tea and coffee.

DINNER.

A Cheap Soup.—Two lbs. lean beef, 6 potatoes, 6 onions parboiled, a carrot, turnip, head of celery, $\frac{1}{2}$ pt. split peas, 4 qts. water, some whole pepper, and a red herring. Boil well, and rub through a coarse sieve. Serve with fried bread.

Boiled Perch.—Boil quickly with salt, then simmer slowly 10 minutes; melted butter and parsley sauce.

Boiled Mutton, butter sauce, with potatoes, onions, turnips, and carrots.

A French Pie.—Lay a puff paste on the edge of a dish, put veal in slices with forcemeat balls, and sweetbreads cut fine. Add mushrooms, seasoning, cover with gravy, a crust, and bake 1 hour.

Dessert.

Hasty Pudding.—One qt. milk, while boiling shake in 2 tablespoonfuls of flour, and stir till it thickens. Put in a deep dish, stir in an oz. of butter, do. sugar, and add grated nutmeg. Sugar sauce.

Floating Island.

Pears, apples, and dates.

Tea, or Lunch.

Cold roast veal, birds stewed and spiced, cold. *Potato Fritters.* (Boil 2 large potatoes, scraped fine, 4 eggs, 1 large spoon of cream, do. wine, a squeeze of lemon, and a little nutmeg. Beat the batter $\frac{1}{2}$ an hour, and fry in boiling lard.) Corn pone, crackers, and cheese, stewed pears, dry toast, bread, tea. *Seed Cake.* ($1\frac{1}{2}$ lbs. flour, 1 lb. sugar, 8 eggs, 1 oz. seeds, 2 spoonfuls yeast, and same of milk.)

THURSDAY.

Breakfast. — Cold rabbit, minced mutton, poached eggs, corn muffins, rice cake, rolls. Tea and coffee.

DINNER.

Spanish Soup.—Three lbs. beef, 1 lb. ham, cover well with water, boil and skim. Add a teaspoonful pepper, simmer 2 hours; cook separately a cup of rice, onions cut small, and cabbage. Eat them separate from the soup if desired.

Roast Oysters.

Roast Veal, with corn, tomatoes, and baked mashed potatoes.

Beef Steak Broiled.

Dessert.

Peach Pie.

Matrimony.—Make ice cream, after the Newport receipt, (1 qt. milk, 1 pt. cream, 2 tablespoons corn starch, and the yolk of one egg, sweeten and flavor to taste; mix the corn starch in part of the milk, and add the egg, then add to the milk, boiling hot. When cool it is ready for the freezer,—and mix with fresh, or canned peaches; freeze all together.)

Grapes, chestnuts, and pears.

TEA, OR LUNCH.

Cold roast beef, pickled tripe, crackers with anchovy, paste spread on them; raspberry jam, corn bread, dry toast. *Sponge Cake.* (Break 10 eggs into a deep pan, with 1 lb. sifted sugar, set the pan into warm water, and beat $\frac{1}{4}$ of an hour, till the batter is thick and warm. Then take out of the water, and whisk till cold. Stir in lightly 1 lb. flour, and flavor with essence of lemon.) Tea and chocolate.

FRIDAY.

Breakfast.—Turkey hash on toast, cold ham, sardines, scallops fried, cream toast, rolls. Tea and coffee.

DINNER.

Game Soup.—Take 2 old birds, or pieces left from the table, cut fine, with 2 slices of ham, 3 lbs. of beef, a piece of celery, and 2 large onions. Put on the fire with 5 pts. of boiling water, and stew gently for 2 hours. Then strain, and put back into the pot with some stewed celery, and fried bread, season well, skim, and serve hot.

Lobster.

Roast Lamb, with cauliflower, oyster plant, and potatoes.

Chicken Pie.— Half boil a large fowl, and cut in pieces; put the broth rich into a deep dish with a handful of parsley scalded in milk, and season well. Add the fowl, and bake with a raised crust. When done, lift the crust, and add $\frac{1}{2}$ pt. cream, scalded, with a little butter and flour in it; mix well with the gravy.

Dessert.

Apple Pie.
Boiled Rice, in cups, with cream and sugar.
Apples, pears, and nuts.

Tea, or Lunch.

Dutch herring, raw oysters, cold hock, milk toast, Graham bread, stewed apples. *Spanish Fritters.* (Cut French rolls into pieces length of a finger, mix together one egg, cream, sugar, and cinnamon, and soak them in it. When well soaked, fry a light brown, and serve with wine and sugar sauce.) Chocolate, cheese.

SATURDAY.

Breakfast.—Beefsteak with mushrooms, cold potted game, fried Indian pudding, sausage, toast, rolls. Tea and coffee.

Dinner.

Venison Soup.—4 lbs. venison cut in small pieces, and stewed gently in brown gravy soup. Strain, and serve with French beans cut in diamonds, adding 2 glasses of port wine; separate from the soup if desired.

Fried Perch.

Roast Turkey, cranberry sauce, with potatoes, beets, and squash.

Irish Stew.—5 thick mutton chops, 2 lbs. potatoes, peeled and cut in halves; 6 onions sliced, and seasoning. Put a layer of potatoes at the bottom of the pan, then a couple of chops, and some onions; then another similar Add 3 gills of gravy, and 2 teasponfuls mushroom catsup. Cover close, and stew 1½ hours. A small slice of ham is an addition.

Dessert.

Baked Apple Dumplings.
Blancmange.
Fruit and nuts.

TEA, OR LUNCH.

Cold tongue, pickled fish, French bread, boiled rice stewed prunes, *Ginger Pound-cake.* (1 lb. butter, do. sugar, do. flour, 8 eggs, and 2 tablespoons yellow ginger.) Tea and coffee.

SUNDAY.

Breakfast.—Cold roast turkey, ham cake, anchovy, toast, fried samp, buckwheat cakes, brown bread, gems. Tea and coffee.

DINNER.

Tomato Soup.—Plain beef soup, with 2 cups of fresh or canned tomatoes, well seasoned.

Boiled Cod, oyster sauce.

Roast Ducks, with currant jelly, sweet potatoes, cauliflower, spinach, and stewed potatoes.

Boiled Ham.

Dessert.

Mince Pie.

Delicate Dish.

Grapes, apples, and almonds.

TEA, OR LUNCH.

Broiled salmon, cold corned beef, Boston crackers, with tomato catsup, waffles, dry toast, preserved grapes, assorted cakes. Tea.

DECEMBER.

MONDAY.

Breakfast.—Fried chicken, cream sauce, potatoes à la maître d' hôtel, baked beans, brown bread. rolls, dry toast. Tea and coffee.

DINNER.

Ox-tail Soup.—Cut up 2 ox-tails, separating them at the joints; fry them with butter, together with 4 lbs. of gravy beef, a carrot, turnip, 3 onions, a leek, a head of celery, and a bunch of sweet herbs; add a pint of water, and a teaspoonful of peppercorns; stir over the fire till the pan is covered with a glaze; fill up the pot with 3 qts. of water, and when it boils set it where it will simmer until the tails are tender, then trim them and lay aside. Cut some turnips and carrots in fancy shapes (about ½ a pt. of the two), 2 doz. button onions, and a head of celery; boil them in a little soup till quite tender; strain off the soup through a fine napkin, add the vegetables and tails, and season with salt, pepper, and a small piece of lump sugar.

Sea-bass, butter sauce.

Broiled Chicken, oyster sauce; with potatoes, cauliflower, and lima beans.

Venison Steak.

Dessert.

Tapioca Pudding.—Simmer 4 oz. tapioca in a pint of milk, ten minutes; then add ½ pt. cream, a teaspoonful pounded cinnamon, 4 oz. butter warmed, same of white sugar, and yolks of 4 eggs well beaten; a little oil of almonds will improve the flavor. Bake half an hour.

Custard Pie.

Pears, grapes, and nuts.

Tea, or Lunch.

Pickled shad, cold mutton, clam fritters (make a batter as for common fritters, and stir in the clams chopped fine), steam toast, crackers, French bread, quince marmalade, cream cake, (1 lb. of flour, do. sugar, 1½ lbs. of butter, ½ pt. milk, 4 eggs, citrons, raisins and spice.)

TUESDAY.

Breakfast.—Cold venison pie, fried scallops, fried sweet potatoes, cream toast, potted fish, rolls. Chocolate and coffee.

Dinner.

Macaroni Soup.—A plain beef soup with Italian macaroni boiled in it.

Frostfish fried.

Roast Beef, with baked potatoes, spinach, and beets.

Chicken Croquettes.—Take the white meat and chop fine, with bread crumbs, sage leaves, pepper and salt, and one egg. Roll into balls and fry.

Dessert.

Plum Pudding.—One lb. stoned raisins, do. currants, do. fresh beef suet chopped fine, 2 oz. sweet almonds, and 1 of bitter, blanched and pounded; mix together with 1 lb. flour, do. bread crumbs, soaked in milk (squeezed dry, and reduced to a mash before mixing with the flour), 2 oz. each of citron, preserved orange and lemon peel, and ½ oz. mixed spice (2 wine-glasses of brandy should be poured over the fruit and spice, mixed together, and allowed to stand 3 or 4 hours before the pudding is made), ¼ lb. moist sugar beaten with 8 eggs; stir all in the pudding, and make it thin enough with milk—consistence of good batter. It must be tied in a cloth, and will take five hours' constant boiling. When done, sift loaf sugar over the top, and serve with wine sauce.

Crême a la vanille.—Boil ½ a stick of vanilla in ¼ pt. of new milk until it has a high flavor; have ready dissolved in water 1 oz. of isinglass, mix with the milk, and 1¼ pts. of fine cream; sweeten with fine sugar, and whip until quite thick, then pour into the mould, and set in a cool place.

Pears, grapes, and nuts.

Tea, or Lunch.

Potted game, sardines, cold chicken, cracker toast, rolls, stewed prunes, breadcake.

WEDNESDAY.

Breakfast.—Veal cutlets, fried scallops, boiled hominy, cold boiled ham, rolls, flour griddle-cakes. Tea and coffee.

Dinner.

Cottage Soup.—Two lbs. lean beef cut into small pieces, ¼ lb. bacon, 2 lbs. mealy potatoes, 3 oz. rice, carrots, turnips, and onions sliced, or leeks and cabbage. Fry the meat, onions and cabbage in butter or dripping, and then put them in a gallon of water, to stew gently for 3 hours, putting in the rice, carrots, and turnips only long enough to allow them to get well done. Mash the potatoes, and pass through a colander, season well, and keep closely covered. It will make 5 pts. of excellent soup, at small cost.

Stewed Eels.—Cut the eels in pieces, fry until brown, then let them cool. Take an onion, some parsley, a sage leaf chopped, and put them in some gravy with a clove, blade of mace, pepper and salt, a glass of port wine, and a little lemon-juice. Strain the sauce, thicken with butter and flour, add a little catsup, and stir the eels until tender.

Roast Lamb, mint sauce, with mashed potatoes baked, macaroni baked with cheese, and turnips.

Cold Quail pâté.

Dessert.

Swiss Pudding.—Put layers of bread crumbs and sliced apples, with sugar between, till the dish is full. Let the crumbs be uppermost, then put butter warmed over it, and bake.

Squash Pie.—One qt. pulp strained, 1 qt. milk, with the squash stirred in when boiling, with two spoonfuls flour, 2 eggs, piece of butter size of an egg, season to taste with sugar, cinnamon, and a little salt.

French chestnuts boiled, and pears.

Tea, or Lunch.

Cold game pie, cold roast beef, fried Indian pudding, toast, blackberry jam, cheese, bread and butter; jelly cake (make three or four *thin* sheets of cup cake, 1 cup butter, 2 of sugar, 3 of flour, and 4 eggs, ½ teaspoonful of soda, and 1 of cream of tartar, latter shaken in the flour dry, and spread with jelly, laying one over the other). Chocolate.

THURSDAY.

Breakfast.—Lamb chops, fried oysters, cold tongue, corn pone, Graham biscuit, rolls. Tea and coffee.

Dinner.

Gravy Soup.—Lean beef in the proportion of 1 pt. water to 1 lb. meat, and 2 oz. of ham; cover with water and simmer for 3 hours, during which time it must not boil, as the pores of the meat will then be opened and the gravy drawn, throw in 3 qts. of warm water, with ¼ oz. each of pepper, allspice, and salt, as well as sweet herbs, cloves, 2 or 3 carrots and turnips, together with 2 heads of celery, and boil all slowly till the meat is done to rags. Strain it well. It will keep well.

Fried Perch.

Roast Chickens, with cauliflower, boiled rice, and sweet potatoes; cranberry sauce.

Calf's Brains, fried in batter.

Dessert.

Lemon Pie.

Charlotte Russe.—Line the bottom of a mold with Savoy biscuits, or sponge cakes, and fill it with any kind of cream, according to taste.

Apples, grapes, and hickory nuts.

Tea, or Lunch.

Ham cake, cold birds, omelet, crackers, corn bread, rolls, stewed pears; cheese cake, ($\frac{1}{4}$ lb. butter, do. sugar, beaten together, 4 eggs, $\frac{1}{2}$ pt. milk with *half* the egg boiled together till it becomes a curd, stirred with a knife, with 2 oz. grated bread thrown in. Stir all into the butter and sugar, with the rest of the egg, and add $\frac{1}{4}$ lb. currants, $\frac{1}{2}$ glass wine or brandy, and teaspoonful of cinnamon, mace, and nutmeg mixed. Bake in a paste $\frac{1}{2}$ an hour.)

FRIDAY.

Breakfast.—Chicken hash, sausage toast, minced salt codfish with potatoes, fried hominy, Indian griddle-cakes, bread and butter, toast. Tea and coffee.

Dinner.

Chicken broth, with rice.
Striped Bass, broiled.

Roast Goose, with apple-sauce, tomatoes, potatoes, and beets; chow-chow pickle.

Broiled Oysters.

Dessert.

Baked Indian Pudding.—Boil a pint of milk, and into it stir 1 cup meal, do. molasses, one teaspoonful salt, first mixed with a little cold milk; boil it, and pour it into a deep earthenware pot, well buttered, and with a pint of cold milk in it; add one egg and a teaspoonful of ginger. Bake in a slow oven.

Wine Jelly.

Oranges, filberts, and dates.

Tea, or Lunch.

Boned turkey, sardines, cold roast chicken, brown bread, milk toast, bread, crackers and cheese, stewed peaches, La Galette cake (1 lb. of flour, do. butter, 2 eggs; knead all into a paste, and make the size of a dessert plate; put in the oven $\frac{1}{4}$ of an hour, then take it out, beat up 2 more eggs with a little cream and salt, pour over the cake, and bake $\frac{1}{4}$ of an hour more).

SATURDAY.

Breakfast.—Cold roast goose, head cheese, corned beef hash, stewed potatoes, steam toast, muffins, bread. Tea and coffee.

Dinner.

Potato Soup.—Take large mealy potatoes, peel and cut in small slices, with an onion; boil in 3 pts. water till tender, and pulp through a colander. Add a small piece of butter, a little cayenne pepper, and salt, and just before the soup is served 2 spoonfuls of good cream. It must not boil after the cream is put in.

Roast Oysters, on toast.

Boiled Corned Beef, with rice croquettes, potatoes, and cabbage.

Partridges roasted; currant jelly.

Dessert.

Peach Pie.

Cream Meringues.—(From the Confectioner.)

Oranges and nuts.

Tea, or Lunch.

Chicken Salad.—(Cut the meat from 2 fowls, boiled or roasted, in pieces not exceeding an inch; white part of 2 large bunches of celery in the same way, mix together, cover, and set away. Mash the yolks of 9 hard boiled eggs to a paste, and mix with $\frac{1}{2}$ pt. sweet oil, do. vinegar, a gill mustard, a teaspoonful cayenne, and one of salt. Stir till well mixed and smooth. Then set away. *Five minutes* before the salad is wanted, pour the dressing on, and mix well). Cold veal, boiled rice, rolls and bread, canned peaches. French Cake—*Bolas d'Amor* (1¼ lbs. flour, 1 cup yeast, ½ pt. milk warmed, 1 lb. butter, 4 eggs. Make a hole in the flour, and pour in the milk, eggs, and yeast. Mix all together, beating in the butter by degrees, and let it stand an hour to rise. Mix in ½ lb. sifted sugar; ornament with citron). Tea and chocolate.

SUNDAY.

Breakfast.—Broiled ham, cold roast pork, chipped potatoes, buckwheat cakes, gems, rolls. Tea and coffee.

DINNER.

Winter Soup.—2 carrots, do. turnips, and the heart of a head of celery. Cut into small pieces with 6 button onions, and half boil in salt and water, with a little sugar, then throw into a rich beef broth. Add small dumplings boiled in water, just before serving.

Fried Trout.

Stewed Chickens—With macaroni stewed, and potatoes. Cut in pieces and scald, fry in butter with sweet herbs chopped, pepper and salt, and add boiling water and flour. Stew until cooked, and add a tablespoon of cream, yolk of an egg, and a little lemon juice.

Quail on Toast.

Dessert.

Batter Pudding.—1 qt. milk, 6 eggs, 14 tablespoons

flour, a little salt. Boil 1 hour and 10 minutes; cold wine sauce.

Brandy Peaches.

Prunes, grapes, and nuts.

Tea, or Lunch.

Cold beef, partridge pâté, steam toast, muffins; preserved plums, bread, tea, cookies (1 cup butter, 2 sugar, 5 flour, 1 egg, 4 tablespoons milk, and spice).

APPENDIX

Pickles and Sauces.—Avoid all use of metal vessels in their preparation, use wooden spoons, and keep in wide-mouthed bottles.

To Pickle small Cucumbers.—Take *one hundred*—in September—place in a deep stone jar, sprinkle with a pint of salt, pour on boiling water, and cover tight, that no steam evaporate. Let them stand twenty-four hours. Wipe each one dry with a cloth.

Place in an unglazed jar, and cover with boiling vinegar, spiced, with cloves, whole pepper and mace. Eat after two weeks. The same proportion for any number.

To Pickle Cauliflower.—Strip off the leaves, quarter the stalk, and scald in salt and water till soft; dry on a sieve, and cut in small pieces after twenty-four hours; place in a jar, and cover with cold spiced vinegar: seal up.

To Pickle Eggs.—Boil hard, twelve or more, and lay into cold water; peel off the shells, and lay whole into a stone jar, with mace, cloves, and nutmegs. Fill up with boiling vinegar, cover close; after three days scald the vinegar again, and pour over; cork tight. Use in two weeks.

To Pickle Mushrooms.— Clean, and place in layers sprinkled with salt, for two days; add whole black pepper and spice; cover close, and set in a cool oven for an hour. Strain off the liquor, and add cloves, mace, and allspice. Let it boil, then throw the mushrooms in, set away till cold, then add a little vinegar, and pot.

To Pickle Walnuts. — Gather about the middle of July; prick with a needle, and put into water for three days, changing the water every day. Make a strong brine of salt and water, boil and skim; when cold, take one gallon to every hundred walnuts. Let them stand six (6) days, change the water, and leave six days more. Drain, and expose to the sun, so they may turn black. Make a strong pickle of wine vinegar, flavored with cloves, mace, whole pepper, mustard-seed, and horse-radish. Allow to every hundred walnuts, six spoonfuls of mustard-seed, with one of whole pepper. They will be good for years; not fit for use for six months, however.

To Pickle Lemons.—Take the finest, with thick rinds; cut incisions, and fill them with salt. Put on a dish, and lay near the fire, or in a hot sun; repeat the operation several times.

Make a pickle of the best of cider vinegar, spiced with cloves, allspice and ginger, and pour over when cold; bottle tight, and keep for years.

Walnut Vinegar. — Put walnut shells into a strong brine for ten days, then lay in the sun for a week to dry. Place in jar, and cover with boiling vinegar. In *ten days* pour it off, and boil again. Then stand for a month, and it will be fit for use; excellent for cold meat, and flavoring sauces.

Cucumber Vinegar.—Pare and slice *fifteen* large ones; place in a stone jar, with *three* pints of vinegar, *four* large onions also sliced, *two* large spoonfuls of salt, *three* teaspoonfuls of pepper, and one half a one of cayenne; after standing four days, boil, and strain when cold, and bottle.

Sauce Universal.—Take one pint mushroom catsup, one glass of port-wine, and a teaspoonful of vinegar, one do. black pepper, salt, allspice, and minced onion. Set it in a jar in water, increasing the heat to 90° Fahrenheit; stand twenty-four hours. Then after one week strain and bottle; a great addition to gravies.

To Flavor Vinegar.—Take any kind of fruit, or herb, and boil in it a short time, and bottle when cold; a great addition to cutlets.

Jersey Pickle.—Slice and chop *one* peck green tomatos, *six* peppers and *four* onions; throw over them *one* cup of salt, and let them stand twenty-four hours; then drain, and put into a stewpan, cover with the best of cider vinegar, stewing slowly. Add *one* cup brown sugar, *two* spoonfuls horse-radish grated, *one* of powdered cloves, *one* of allspice, *one* of cinnamon, and boil full three hours; bottle in wide-mouthed jar, and seal.

Chile Sauce.—*Three* peppers chopped fine, seeds included; *one* large onion, *twelve* ripe tomatoes, peeled; *one* tablespoonful of salt, *one* of sugar, *one* teaspoonful of allspice, do. cloves, do. ginger, do. nutmeg, *two* tea-cups of best of vinegar; boil well one hour and bottle.

Tomato Catsup.— One gallon of skinned tomatoes, boiled and strained; then add, *four* tablespoonfuls of salt, *four* tablespoons of black pepper, *two* of allspice, *two* of cinnamon ½ one of red pepper pure, one quart wine vinegar; boil well one hour, bottle and seal, when cold. Keep in a dry place.

Mushroom Catsup.—Break up the mushrooms, scraping off the dirt with a knife; place in layers in an earthen pan, sprinkling with salt. Cover the pan with a towel, for twenty four hours, rub them up, and strain through a muslin, squeezing out all the juice. To every quart add *one* tablespoonful of black peppers, whole, *one* teaspoonful of allspice, *one* half do. of cayenne, *one* dozen cloves, and *four* large blades of mace; boil slowly four hours, pour into a bowl or deep dish to settle for twenty-four hours, covered. Then pour gently through a fine hair-seive, and put into small bottles, putting in the top of each one a few drops of olive-oil and sealing the cork; it will keep for years, in a cool place.

Preserves and Confectionery.—Every article of this kind should be made of the best of sugar, and small fruits for jams, previously boiled to evaporate the watery particles, before adding the requisite amount. The following is the best method we have seen for preserving fruit.

Melt one pound of sugar in one half-pint of water, and put into every quart-bottle of fruit. Place the bottles in boiler, or steaming-box, in cold water, raising the heat to boiling point: have ready corks steamed so as to be flexible, force them by blows from a mallet. Pare the corks close to the bottle. Have ready a vessel of melted sealing wax, of the following ingredients: One pound of rosin, three ounces beeswax, one and a half of tallow; have ready a brush, and cover the corks, then dip the mouth into the melted wax; then transfer it to a cold basin of water. Repeat the operation, and see that the wax is smooth and complete. Pack away in a cool, dry cellar, excluding all light. Examine after one week, to see if there were flaws in the bottle; or any marks of fermentation. Peaches and pears should be dropped into cold water, to prevent their color changing after paring.

To Keep Grapes in Brandy.—Take large, close bunches, black or white; lay them in a jar, put the weight of them in powdered sugar over them, and cover with brandy. Tie down with a bladder; prick the grapes with a pin, first.

To preserve Strawberries in Wine.—Put large fine ones in a wide-mouthed bottle, strew over with fine sugar, fill up with Madeira wine or Sherry.

To preserve Oranges or Lemons in Jelly.—Make a hole the size of a shilling, and scrape the pulp out clean; lay in soft water for two days, then boil tender, slowly; to every pound of fruit, take two of sugar, and one pint of water; boil with the juice to a syrup, then boil the fruit in the syrup half an hour.

Marmalades.—Boil ripe apricots in syrup; beat in a mortar, take half their weight in loaf sugar, and water to dissolve it; boil well together till thick.

Orange Compote.—Lay the oranges in water four hours, boil till tender, cut in halves, and take out the insides; to every pound of peel, *well pounded,* add one of sugar; take out the seeds, add the weight in sugar to that, and beat; mix and pot.

To dry Cherries without Sugar.—Stone, and set them over the fire, letting them simmer in their own liquor; let them get cold; give them another scald, and spread on sieves to dry, in a cool oven.

Orange Syrup.—Take large, deep-coloured oranges, and throw into water for twelve hours; put into a cloth and boil, cut in quarters; and after taking out the pulp, throw into cold water. Make a thick syrup, and add the pulp.

Colouring for Jellies.—For *yellow*, yolk of eggs, or a bit of saffron steeped in the liquid. For *green*, spinach leaves, or beet leaves. For *red*, beet root sliced.

Bonbons.—Clear off the sugar from fresh candied citron; cut into squares one inch thick, stick on a bit of wire, and dip into liquid syrup; wet a dish with a few drops of pure olive oil, and lay the fruit to cool.

Toffie.—Melt in a stewpan, three ounces of butter, add one pound of moist sugar, stir well over a slow fire, boil one quarter of an hour; pour out on buttered dishes, and mark in squares.

Candied Fruit.—When boiled in the syrup, put a

layer on a new sieve, and dip it suddenly into hot water, drain, and cover with sifted sugar; dry in a warm oven, turning over frequently.

Raspberry or Blackberry Vinegar.—Take a jar of vinegar and fill with fruit; let it stand for three days: strain, and for every pint of juice, add one pound of sugar; boil up once, and skim; bottle and seal.

FINIS.

COMPANION TO IRVING'S WASHINGTON.

GEN. GREENE'S LIFE.—The Life of Nathaniel Greene, Major-General in the Army of the Revolution. By Geo. Washington Greene, author of Historical View of the American Revolution. 3 vols. 8vo. University Press. The first volume will be ready Dec. 10. Price to Subscribers, $4 per volume.

The history of the United States is naturally divided into three parts:

1. The history of their foundation, or their Colonial history; 2. The history of their transition from colonial to independent national life, or the history of the Revolution; 3. The history of their constitutional life, or the history of the growth of the Union. A thorough knowledge of each of these periods is essential to a just comprehension of the whole. The seeds of the Revolution must be sought in our Colonial history. The history of our life as a nation loses both its philosophical and its practical importance if separated from the history of the Revolution. A careful study of the War of Independence would have saved us thousands of lives and millions of money in the War of the Rebellion. Next to the life of Washington, it is in the life of Greene that this history is to be sought; nor can it be fully understood without reading both. It is in the hope of contributing to the materials for this study, and in the conviction that to preserve the memory of great and good men is one of the highest offices of patriotism, that these volumes are offered to the student of American history.

"The first volume of the biography is a very handsome octavo volume of nearly six hundred pages, printed in the best style of the University Press. It brings Gen. Greene's life down to the year 1778. The style is clear, simple, vigorous, readily adapting itself to the varied demands of description, reflection, and narrative, and betraying on every page that unnamable peculiarity which indicates that the labor of composition is literally a labor of love, and that the biographer is writing from a full heart as well as from a full mind."—*Boston Transcript.*

TUCKERMAN'S BOOK OF THE ARTISTS. 8vo, cloth, $5. Large paper, $12.00.

"No American author is better fitted than Mr. Tuckerman for the task he has undertaken and so ably executed."—*N. Y. Times.*

"As a book of general information about American art and artists, Mr. Tuckerman's book will be found both valuable and interesting."—*Brooklyn Union.*

"Mr. Tuckerman, than whom no writer could bring to the consideration of his subject more diligence or a more hearty love of art, has prepared a compendium of the history of American painting and sculpture, which supplies a want in our literature. His Book of the Artists is a full and interesting record of the progress of Art in the United States."—*Evening Post.*

NEW AND IMPORTANT EDUCATIONAL WORK.

FAY'S GREAT OUTLINE OF GEOGRAPHY FOR HIGH SCHOOLS AND FAMILIES. The text-book in 12mo; the Atlas in large folio. Retail price, $3.75; Library edition, in cloth, $4.25. Liberal terms for schools. Teachers supplied with a copy for examination at half price.

"The author of this work presents the public with an entirely new system of studying Geography. We confess the plan strikes us with great favor. Without disparaging other text-books, we must say, this seems to us to be more exactly adapted to its purpose than any. * * * * The mechanical execution of the Atlas deserves strong praise. If you have a child who is hard to learn Geography, or one who wishes to learn it easier, or if you wish to undertake a résumé of your own knowledge, or add to what you already know, Fay's system is the way to do it, and his Great Outline the means. The most stupid will find that knowledge would be instilled into them in spite of themselves."—*Albany Evening Journal.*

"The treatise of Mr. Fay is complete in itself. He gives a well-constructed Atlas of the globe, and with it a little manual containing a series of lessons on the maps, with occasional illustrative comments. This careful map-study, embracing physical as well as political characteristics, may serve either as an introduction to geography or as a final review or résumé of one's knowledge. In either case it is adapted to the older scholars of our ordinary schools. The plan which it proposes seems to us very well carried out; and simple as the 'Outline' at first appears, we have been surprised to discover its comprehensiveness and completeness. Obviously the book may be used advantageously before or after other books. There is one feature of the book which has particularly interested us, bearing, as we presume, the impress of Mr. Fay's long acquaintance with German schools. It is intended that the scholar shall learn his lessons under the eye and with the aid of his teacher, who is to *drill* the class. Most of our American teachers do not teach, but hear recitations. Mr. Fay would have them go over each lesson with the class, and see that all its contents are mastered.

"Mr. Fay's maps and text are brought down to the latest moment. Alaska belongs to the United States, the reconstructed North Germany is delineated, and the statistics are gathered from Behm's admirable 'Hand-book,' and other recent publications."—*The Nation, N. Y.*

"BOSTON, December 24.
"The Atlas is better in execution than any School Atlas I have ever seen."
—W. P. ATKINSON, *Prof. in Mass. Inst. of Technology.*

"Fay's Geography seems to meet a want not met by any existing works, and its execution is highly creditable to author and publishers."—ABNER J. PHIPPS, *Agent of Mass. Board of Education.*

"Of the mechanical part of the work, maps, printing, etc., there can be but one opinion. Nothing of the kind yet published surpasses it."—EBEN S. STEARNS, *N. Y. State Normal School, Albany.*

"I think Mr. Fay's Geography ought to supersede all others now in use. The opinion of Baron von Humboldt is enough to stamp its value anywhere."
—JOHN CATLIN.

NATURAL THEOLOGY; or, Nature and the Bible from the same Author. Lectures delivered before the Lowell Institute, Boston. By P. A. Chadbourne, A.M., M.D., President of University of Wisconsin. 12mo, cloth, $2.00. Student's edition, $1.75.

"This is a valuable contribution to current literature, and will be found adapted to the uses of the class-room in college, and to the investigations of private students."—*Richmond Christian Adv.*

"The warm, fresh breath of pure and fervent religion pervades these eloquent pages."—*Am. Baptist.*

"Prof. Chadbourne's book is among the few mataphysical ones now published, which, once taken up, cannot be laid aside unread. It is written in a perspicuous, animated style, combining depth of thought and grace of diction, with a total absence of ambitious display."—*Washington National Republican.*

"In diction, method, and spirit, the volume is attractive and distinctive to a rare degree."—*Boston Traveller.*

BENEDICITE; or, Illustrations of the Power, Wisdom, and Goodness of God in the Creation. By G. Chaplin Child, M.D. 12mo, cloth, extra, gilt top, $2.50; red edges, $2.50; gilt edges, $3.00; morocco antique, $5.00.

"Written in an easy and flowing style, abounding in illustrations and incidents, the book cannot fail to interest as well as instruct. The getting-up of the volume is exceedingly tasteful and elegant."—*Journal and Messenger.*

"The most admirable popular treatise of natural theology. It is no extravagance to say that we have never read a more charming book, or one which we can recommend more confidently to our readers with the assurance that it will aid them, as none that we know of can do, to

'Look through Nature up to Nature's God.'

Every clergyman would do well particularly to study this book. For the rest, the handsome volume is delightful in appearance, and is one of the most creditable specimens of American book-making that has come from the Riverside Press."—*Round Table, N. Y.*, June 1.

THE GHOST—A STORY. By W. D. O'Connor. With two illustrations by Nast. 16mo, $1.25; gilt edges, $1.50.

"Told with a tender-heartedness and naturalness of style which are certain to make it a favorite."—*Brooklyn Union.*

"Rich in sweetness, pathos, and tender humanity."—*Providence Journal.*

"If he has other stories of this sort, we beg him to bring them to light without delay."—*Boston Watchman.*

Alvord, and bound in rich morocco, by Matthews In one quarto volume, morocco, $18.00; half mor., gilt top, $16.00; cloth, full gilt, $15.00.

IRVING'S TRAVELLER. Tales of a Traveller. By Geoffrey Crayon, Gent. Author's revised edition. In one volume. Sunnyside Ed. 12mo., $2.50. Illust. ed. 12mo., mor., $6,00, 8vo., $8.00. Riverside Edition, 16mo., $1.75; full gilt, $2.00.

Has always been one of the most popular of Irving's productions, and is not destined to lose the place it so soon acquired in the estimation of the world.—*Boston Traveller.*

IRVING'S WOLFERT'S ROOST. Wolfert's Roost and other Papers, now first collected by Washington Irving. In one volume, 12mo. Sunnyside Edition, cloth, $2.50. Riverside Edition, cloth, $1.75.

The papers in the present volume are among his latest and most charming productions.—*Chicago Tribune.*

MAGA STORIES. Comprising Seventeen Notable Stories of varied character and lively interest, chiefly from *Putnam's Monthly.* 16mo. paper, 75 cts.; cloth extra, bevelled, $1.25.

MAGA SOCIAL PAPERS.—" Pithy and entertaining;" On a variety of topics relating to Society, Manners, Customs, and Habits of the time. By several hands. First contributed to *Putnam's Monthly.* 16mo. paper, 75 cts.; cloth extra, bevelled, gilt tops, $1.25.

MAGA EXCURSION PAPERS. Including Seventeen spirited and lively Sketches of Travel in two hemispheres and elsewhere. 16mo. paper, 75 cts.; cloth extra, bevelled, $1.25.

MAGA PAPERS ON PARIS. By H. T. Tuckerman. 16mo. paper, 60 cts.; cloth extra, $1.00.

⁎ The above volumes are neatly printed in new and legible type, and will be found to be capital books for the fireside and for travellers.

"The delight of childhood, the chivalric companion of refined womanhood, the solace of life at every period; his writings are an imperishable legacy of grace and beauty to his countrymen."

NEW EDITIONS OF IRVING'S WORKS.

THREE EDITIONS ISSUED MONTHLY.

I. *THE KNICKERBOCKER EDITION.*—Large 12mo, on superfine laid paper, with Illustrations, elegantly printed from new stereotype plates, and bound in extra cloth, gilt top. Price to subscribers for the whole set, $2.25 per vol. Half calf, extra, $3.75.

⁎ This edition will be sold only to subscribers for the whole set. It is the *best* edition for libraries and for the centre-table.

II. *THE RIVERSIDE EDITION.*—16mo, on fine white paper; from new stereotype plates; green crape cloth, gilt top, bevelled edges, $1.75 per vol.

III. *THE PEOPLE'S EDITION.*—From the same stereotype plates as above, but printed on cheaper paper, neatly bound in cloth; price, $1.25 per vol.

The issue of the above several editions was commenced October 1, 1867. A volume will be issued punctually on the first day of each month, until the whole series is completed, in the following order:

Bracebridge Hall (Ready).	Goldsmith (April).	Granada.
Wolfert's Roost, "	Alhambra (May).	Salmagundi.
Sketch Book, "	Columbus, 3 vols.	Spanish Papers.
Traveller, "	Astoria.	Miscellanies.
Knickerbocker (Feb.).	Bonneville.	Washington, 5 vols.
Crayon Miscellany (Mar.).	Mahomet, 2 vols.	Life and Letters, 4 vols.

The re-issue of these works in their several forms is unusually elegant. The plates are new, the paper superior, the printing elegant, and each, in proportion to price, combining good taste with economy.

Putnam's Monthly Magazine

OF

LITERATURE, SCIENCE, ART,

AND

NATIONAL INTERESTS.

The re-issue of Putnam's Magazine has been hailed with acclamation in every section of the country, and the publishers are gratified at being able to acknowledge almost innumerable expressions of pleasure and good-will from readers and friends of the first series of "Putnam's Monthly." It is their purpose, in their new enterprise, to leave nothing undone to meet the expectations and desires of the public.

Putnam's Magazine will be a NATIONAL PUBLICATION, supported by the best writers, in each department, from every section of the country. High toned papers on matters of NATIONAL INTEREST, POPULAR SCIENCE, INDUSTRIAL PURSUITS, and sound INFORMATION and INSTRUCTION on important topics, will be especially cultivated. In the lighter articles, healthy entertainment and PURE AMUSEMENT for the family circle will be carefully chosen from the ample resources presented by a large circle of contributors.

TERMS:

$4.00 per Annum in Advance, or 35 cents per number. Two copies to one address, $7.00; three copies to one address, $10.00; ten copies to one address, $30.00. Putnam's Magazine and *Riverside Magazine* for Young People (price $2.50) for $5.50; Putnam's Magazine and *The Round Table* (price $6.00) for $8.00. Or with any other Journal or Magazine in the same proportion.

Special Premiums for Clubs.

G. P. PUTNAM & SON, PUBLISHERS,
661 BROADWAY, NEW YORK.

CPSIA information can be obtained
at www.ICGtesting.com
Printed in the USA
LVHW112106090919
630430LV00002B/338/P